SMALL STREAMS BIG RIVERS

TOM WALKER

Scripture Union
130 City Road, London EC1V 2NJ.

© Tom Walker 1991

First published 1991
by Scripture Union
130 City Road, London EC1V 2NJ

British Library Cataloguing in Publication Data
Walker, Tom
  Small streams, big rivers
  1. Christianity. Religious life
  I. Title
  248.4

ISBN 0 86201 539 1

Scripture quotations in this publication are from the Holy Bible, New International Version. Copyright © 1973, 1978, 1984 International Bible Society. Published by Hodder & Stoughton.

Phototypeset by Intype, London.
Printed and bound in Great Britain by Cox & Wyman Ltd, Reading.

Contents

Abuse of community
Authoritarianism
Rivalry and gossip
Insecurity

Preface

This book has grown out of nearly twenty-one years of ministry at St John's, Harborne. In that time, hundreds of leaders of a variety of small home groups, young people's groups, music groups, dance groups and old people's groups, have worked together. Not all the small groups described in this book enjoyed total success at all times. The experiment relating to Community Groups was important during a time of special mission and outreach, but could not be continued because of over-busy schedules.

But if some small streams have dried up, others have swelled the big river. Through our many small groups we have learnt to share the gospel with our friends and fellow Christians, and we have been strengthened by their fellowship to live it out. I feel very much like Goethe, who said there would be little left of him if he were to 'discard what he owed to others'.

Having left St John's for a new ministry in Nottingham, I can only express gratitude for the experiences in Birmingham that have produced this testimony. My successor's call is to build on what he finds and I pray that he, too, will benefit from Harborne's creative small groups.

Tom Walker

1
Small groups: key to growth

T R Glover said that the secret of the success of the early Christians was that they 'out-lived, out-thought and out-died' the pagan world.

There are those in the church today who see this initial period of the church's growth as the 'ideal' manifestation of the church's life, evidencing patterns and priorities to which we should all conform today. Undoubtedly there are lessons of zeal and enthusiasm from which we can learn, but it is hard to argue that the early church succeeded simply because it had a perfect structure. To talk of structures in the early church is to use too formal a word. The first Christians did not set out to build an organisation. Rather, they saw an *organism* grow as the Spirit of God, poured out at Pentecost, worked and moved among them. The dynamic for their success was the Spirit of God moving in power – not bright ideas, busy activity or good planning. However, without desiring merely to emulate their organisation we can consider and learn from some of the key factors in their growth.

Family

If we look to the Bible, it is clear that the family is the fundamental unit in God's plan for human growth and development. Right back to the moment when 'The Lord God said, "It is not good for man to be alone. I will make a helper suitable for him" ' (Genesis 2:18), there has been an acknowledgement of humanity's need to live interdependently not independently.

The family unit in the Old Testament was important for learning God's ways. As Moses prepared the people of Israel for entering the Promised Land, telling them that he would not cross the Jordan himself but would die before they took possession of the land, he stressed the importance of family instruction so that God's people would continue to obey him and not turn away to idolatry. 'Only be careful, and watch yourselves closely so that you do not forget the things your eyes have seen or let them slip from your heart as long as you live. Teach them to your children and to their children after them' (Deuteronomy 4:9). Following the giving of the Law, parents were again urged to teach their children so that each succeeding generation could learn to obey. 'These are the commands, decrees and laws the Lord your God directed me to teach you to observe in the land that you are crossing the Jordan to possess, so that you, your children and their children after them may fear the Lord your God as long as you live by keeping all his decrees and commands that I give you, and so that you may enjoy long life' (Deuteronomy 6:1-2). The family was the basic small unit in the Old Testament for instruction in God's Law and for learning the lessons of life through corporate human experience.

This is again made clear in the later history of the Israelites when, after the people's return to Jerusalem from captivity in Babylon, Ezra and Nehemiah introduced reforms. The wall of the city had been rebuilt, despite great opposition from the enemies of God's people, and then families were re-registered. The 'heads of families' were prominent both in giving money towards the cost of resettlement, and in re-instructing the people in the standards of God's law. 'On the second day of the month, the heads of all the families, along with the priests and the Levites, gathered around Ezra the scribe to give attention to the words of the Law. They found written in the Law which the Lord had commanded through Moses, that the Israelites were to live in booths during the feast of the seventh month and that they should proclaim this word and spread it throughout their towns and in

Jerusalem' (Nehemiah 8:13–15). The teaching of the Law was restored and the feasts re-established, 'and their joy was very great' (v 17). For this to happen there was the primary, visionary leadership of Ezra and Nehemiah, the formalised teaching role of the priests and Levites, but also the smaller grouping of natural families in which the family heads clearly had a leadership and teaching task.

A new family group

In the New Testament the natural family is presented in a different light. In the Gospels the call of Jesus is sometimes directly in conflict with the call of natural family duty and involvement. Obedience to the call of the kingdom of God is the first priority. It was so for Jesus himself when, aged twelve, he stayed behind in the temple at Jerusalem 'sitting among the teachers, listening to them and asking them questions' (Luke 2:46). At first he received a mild rebuke from Mary, ' "Son, why have you treated us like this? Your father and I have been anxiously searching for you." "Why were you searching for me?" he asked. "Didn't you know I had to be in my Father's house?" But they did not understand what he was saying to them' (Luke 2:48–50). Interestingly, we are told that, after this, 'he went down to Nazareth with them and was obedient to them.' For Jesus, the family was the place in which to learn God's ways by submission in human relationships, but also the place in which to live out the tension of following a higher call, that of direct obedience to his Father in heaven.

This was the demand he made of others too. To the man who wanted to delay following Jesus until the death of his father, Jesus said, 'Let the dead bury their own dead, but you go and proclaim the kingdom of God.' When another said 'I will follow you, Lord; but first let me go and say good-bye to my family,' Jesus replied, 'No-one who puts his hand to the plough and looks back is fit for service in the kingdom of God' (Luke 9:59–62). When a woman in the crowd that was gathered round Jesus called out, 'Blessed is the mother who gave you birth and nursed you,' he replied, 'Blessed rather are those who hear the word of God and obey it' (Luke 11:27–28).

Instead of promising a new sense of family peace and ordered relationships, Jesus taught that he could bring division even to the primary small group unit that God has prepared for man's well-being since the first days of his creation. 'Do you think I came to bring peace on earth? No, I tell you, but division. From now on there will be five in one family divided against each other, three against two and two against three. They will be divided, father against son and son against father, mother against daughter and daughter against mother, mother-in-law against daughter-in-law and daughter-in-law against mother-in-law' (Luke 12:51–53). As a person follows Jesus wholeheartedly and seeks to obey God in kingdom relationships, he will find that this commitment is sometimes in tension with the natural family commitment. Although God put us in families, and it is clear from Old Covenant patterns that the natural family was a primary teaching and learning unit, the rule of God brought in by Jesus establishes a new structure within human society. Membership of the family unit under the terms of the Old Covenant was established by birth, belief and obedience, and it was sealed with the blood shed in circumcision. Thus the head of a Jewish family could make his appeal, 'We are a covenant people, God's people, we all belong to him and we all go his way.' Membership of the kingdom of God is established by virtue of a relationship to Jesus. His first call in the earliest Gospel account was, 'The time has come . . . The kingdom of God is near. Repent and believe the good news!' (Mark 1:15.) To respond to the call of Jesus with repentance from sin and faith in his offer of forgiveness is to 'hear and receive his word', which is the essence of belonging to the kingdom (Mark 4:20). Such kingdom membership is sealed with his blood on the cross, since Jesus had to die to make possible such a relationship with God.

The first small groups of disciples
At first these new relationships with God and with other followers of Christ are pictured for us in the band of disciples whom Jesus called out for special instruction. We think primarily of the group of twelve, one of whom was a traitor. They were intended to be both an embryo of the kingdom of God, and also a blueprint for

later relationships in the church once the Holy Spirit had been outpoured at Pentecost. They were, in a sense, a replacement family. They were the basic minimum small-group structure amongst whom kingdom relationships had to be worked out. But they were not the only grouping.

Within the twelve Jesus clearly had moments of special instruction for an inner core of three – Peter, James and John. They were the three to receive the special insight into the power of Jesus to raise the dead when he went to the home of Jairus, the synagogue ruler, whose daughter had died. 'He did not let anyone follow him except Peter, James and John the brother of James' (Mark 5:37). Jesus chose the same three to witness his transfiguration: 'his clothes became dazzling white, whiter than anyone in the world could bleach them. And there appeared before them Elijah and Moses, who were talking with Jesus' (Mark 9:3–4). Again, in his special teaching for these three there were hints of resurrection, which they were not yet ready to understand. 'As they were coming down the mountain, Jesus gave them orders not to tell anyone what they had seen until the Son of Man had risen from the dead. They kept the matter to themselves, discussing what "rising from the dead" meant' (Mark 9:9–10). When Jesus had to face up to the cost of obedience to his Father's will in the garden of Gethsemane, Peter, James and John were again his specially chosen companions (Mark 14:32–42).

As well as working with an inner group of three disciples, it seems that Jesus had a special bond with John; John speaks of himself as 'the disciple whom Jesus loved' (John 19:26; 21:7). The intimate friendship Jesus developed with John proved to be the basis for working out the new principle of family commitment within the kingdom relationships. We read that from the cross, 'When Jesus saw his mother there, and the disciple whom he loved standing near by, he said to his mother, "Dear woman, here is your son," and to the disciple, "Here is your mother." From that time on, this disciple took her into his home.' (John 19:26–27.) In his teaching Jesus warned that discipleship could be divisive as far as the natural family unit is concerned. In his death, the new harmony of relationship among those 'who hear the word of God and obey it' (Luke 11:28) is established, right at the heart of his own small group of family and disciples.

Many Christians feel almost guilty at the depth of relationship they form with other believers compared with the superficial dealing they have with their own brothers, sisters, uncles, aunts and cousins. However, it is clear that Jesus has brought to us a new quality of love relationship. As he has reconciled us to God by his death 'making peace through his blood, shed on the cross' (Colossians 1:20), so he has made possible a new depth of human love relationship between those who are brothers and sisters in Christ. This is what any small group of believers should discover and express. The small group is not just a convenient structure for organising Christian meetings within the life of the church. It is a God-given way of believers living out the kingdom relationships which Jesus has made possible. It is a fundamental way of expressing the new family commitment that has become possible in Christ. The small-group principle, pioneered by the disciples of Jesus, allows the expression of a love relationship and obedience to Jesus the King, in a way that is impossible for a larger gathering of Christians.

Larger discipleship groups

That is not to say there is no place for the larger group. Jesus gave special powers of apostolic ministry to the seventy disciples he sent out in mission. It is clear from Luke 10 that these were trusted disciples drawn from the crowds who gathered around the twelve, listening to Jesus' teaching. Theirs was no easy task. They were to go out 'like lambs among wolves' (Luke 10:3) and every action and attitude was to convey the urgency of their task. 'Do not take a purse or bag or sandals, and do not greet anyone on the road' (v 4). But perhaps the hardest task was to represent Jesus adequately. He 'sent them two by two ahead of him to every town and place where he was about to go' (v 1). By their behaviour they made it easier or more difficult for Jesus to move into someone's life. Theirs was also a kingdom task: 'When you enter a town and are welcomed, eat what is set before you. Heal the sick who are there and tell them "The kingdom of God is near you" ' (vs 8–9). After the mission was over they 'returned with joy and said, "Lord, even the demons submit to us in your name" ' (v 17). Jesus almost crushed their enthusiasm by putting their earthly success into an eternal context: 'do not rejoice that the spirits submit to you, but rejoice that your names are written in heaven' (v 20).

Even within the larger grouping they ministered in pairs so that they had the strength and encouragement of togetherness in the task. But, clearly, the main purpose of the bigger unit of disciples was to put into effect the lessons learnt in the more intimate sharing of the small group.

In addition to the seventy there were other wider groupings – at times huge crowds listened to Jesus and appeared to welcome his teaching. And among those crowds were people who became genuine disciples but were never included in the more intimate body of disciples. Jesus' ministry was exercised among groups of people who had varying degrees of trust and understanding, and it was partly because of the impossibility of conveying God's truth to people with such widespread needs and such differing attitudes of faith, that the small group was needed for reflection and for more intimate instruction. This is shown clearly in the incident that occurred just after the transfiguration of Jesus. The disciples came down from the vivid mountain-top experience of seeing Christ in his full glory, to meet a situation of desperate human need. There was a demonised boy who had fits and who frequently tried to damage himself by throwing himself into the fire. His father was at his wits' end, crying out for help. Those disciples who had not gone with Jesus onto the mountain, gathered around the boy and tried to cast out the demon – but without success. Watching, cynically, were some scribes and Pharisees, and beyond them the enquiring and casually interested crowd. To all the onlookers the disciples represented failure; only when Jesus came on the scene was the problem solved and the demonised boy delivered. When the boy had been healed, Jesus then took the small group of disciples aside, to give them space for reflection and to teach them that their failure was due to a lack of prayer.

Togetherness

In many respects the togetherness of the disciples around Jesus set the pattern for the early church. Jesus had promised that when two of three were gathered in his name, he would be in the midst of them (Matthew 18:20) and, to their surprise, the disciples found this literally to be the case after Jesus was raised from the dead. John makes a special note of the fact that Jesus appeared to them when 'Simon Peter, Thomas (called Didymus), Nathanael from Cana in Galilee, the sons of Zebedee, and two other disciples were together' (John 21:2). On that occasion Jesus called his followers back from an excursion into their old way of life. Simon Peter had urged them back to fishing, and the others had forgotten that Jesus had called them to be 'fishers of men' (Matthew 4:19). Within the small group the insights of people of different temperaments and spiritual vision are perceived and communicated to others. John, with the bond of a special relationship of love between him and his Lord, was the first to recognise Jesus. Peter, forever open-hearted and even brash in his response to Jesus, was the first in the sea, dashing towards the Lord with a spontaneity of response that took him ahead of all the others. They simply 'followed in the boat, towing the net full of fish' (John 21:8).

The episode with Thomas further illustrates the value of the small group of believers in sustaining others during times of difficulty and doubt. Just as the immediate response of John and Peter communicated to the other disciples, so the testimony of the whole group challenged the unbelief of Thomas. They were full of excitement as they told Thomas that Jesus had appeared to them (John 20:25). Thomas, not having seen that, remained unconvinced but he was at least stimulated by the bold testimony of his friends to commit himself to a public statement of his doubt: 'Unless I see the nail marks in his hands and put my fingers where the nails were, and put my hand into his side, I will not believe it' (John 20:25). He had only to wait a week in doubt and unbelief. The Lord appeared, Thomas saw the scars and surrendered his life. At one level this was because of the way

God dealt with him, not forcing a commitment before Thomas was ready for it. At another level it shows the value of belonging to a group of disciples. We are touched by the experience of Jesus that others have and, in time, their testimony becomes part of ours. Although Thomas' statement was one of doubt, it was witnessed by others as a promise. He could not hold back from surrender to Jesus once he had touched the scars without going back on his word. He was held to the glimmer of faith that shone through his doubting words.

After Jesus ascended to heaven, the togetherness of the disciples was not just a continuing of the old companionship which they had known when Jesus was with them. It was now an expectant togetherness. Jesus had told them to wait in Jerusalem until they had been 'clothed with power from on high' (Luke 24:49). Much of the time was spent in prayer, expecting an imminent divine intervention as a result of Jesus' promise. He had said, 'Do not leave Jerusalem, but wait for the gift my Father promised, which you have heard me speak about. For John baptised with water, but in a few days you will be baptised with the Holy Spirit' (Acts 1:4–5). We read that 'they all joined together constantly in prayer, along with the women and Mary the mother of Jesus, and his brothers' (v 14).

On the day of Pentecost 'they were all together in one place' (Acts 2:1), which meant that all the disciples 'were filled with the Holy Spirit and began to speak in other tongues as the Spirit enabled them' (v 4). Togetherness is the keynote in the verses which describe the fellowship and worship of the Spirit-filled believers. 'They devoted themselves to the apostles' teaching and to the fellowship, to the breaking of bread and to prayer. Everyone was filled with awe, and many wonders and miraculous signs were done by the apostles. All the believers were together and had everything in common' (Acts 2:42–44). The fellowship was both spiritual and social as 'they broke bread in their homes and ate together with glad and sincere hearts, praising God and enjoying the favour of all the people' (vs 46–47).

Their togetherness was strategically important as opposition grew. Peter and John were brought before the authorities and questioned about the healing of the crippled man at the Temple gate. After the hearing they were commanded 'not to speak or teach at all in the name of Jesus' (Acts 4:18). Peter and John knew that they had to obey God, not men, and said, 'we cannot help speaking about what we have seen and heard' (v 20). They were in a quandary but, instead of merely discussing the problem and arriving at a human answer, they 'went back to their own people and reported all that the chief priests and elders had said to them. When they heard this, they raised their voices together in prayer to God' (v 24). The prayer that followed put their predicament into a scriptural context and led to a fresh outpouring of the Spirit of God. Interestingly, the group of disciples were led to a specific prayer topic as they laid the matter before God: 'Lord, consider their threats and enable your servants to speak your word with great boldness' (v 29). As they looked to God for power to testify they prayed, 'Stretch out your hand to heal and perform miraculous signs and wonders through the name of your holy servant Jesus' (v 30).

This togetherness was fundamental to the life of the first Christians. 'All the believers were one in heart and mind' (Acts 4:32) and this sense of unity perfectly answered the High Priestly prayer of Jesus in John 17 when he asked 'that all of them may be one, Father, just as you are in me and I am in you' (v 21). Consequently, it must be the primary characteristic of our small groups today. We cannot recapture the degree of the Spirit's working in power. His intervention at that point in history was a unique part of God's eternal plan. Nor can we be an exact replica of those first Christians who were eye-witnesses of the resurrection of Jesus, and some of whom had spent three special years in his company. But we can match their dedication. We can put such priority on our togetherness in the various groupings of our church life that we find ourselves directed by the Spirit of God to lives of sharing and love. When we meet we can be as directly led in choosing our prayer topics as they were. Unfortunately our meetings are often lethargic and casual, our attendance undisciplined and intermittent. We turn out when we choose to and when it is convenient. There is a lack of urgency and of true godly purpose to our lives.

Open to God in prayer and praise

An attempt to rediscover this immediacy of relationship with God and with fellow Christians that is so characteristic of the New Testament church was made in our 'Open to God' experiment at St John's, Harborne, in the early seventies. (See *Renew us by your Spirit*, Tom Walker; Hodder & Stoughton.) The precise aim of the gathering was to emulate the togetherness of the first disciples in believing prayer, fellowship and study, without rejecting the normal framework of our Anglican church structure. We did not want a return to New Testament patterns and structures simply for their own sake. We still call our small groups 'Open to God' groups, in order to put into effect the vision that we felt was originally given to us by God.

The aim was that every praying Christian who was willing to seek God's will for the future of our church in the suburbs of Birmingham should meet together in prayer and Bible study, until we all sensed that God's will for the future was clearly perceived. 'What's special in that?' someone might ask. 'It sounds no different from any other prayer time held in countless churches all over the world.' The difference for us was that the meeting challenged an existing time of prayer and Bible study. The one represented a standard, totally sincere, well meant, traditional church prayer meeting, attended by the spiritually-minded core of the church. The problem with such meetings is usually their piety! It 'feels' like a meeting only for the élite or for the spiritually advanced. In some churches it can seem to consist of a gathering of the minister's cheer leaders – of people who want to curry favour with the leadership. Such meetings are often heavily dominated by the pastor and do not allow for others to share in ministry.

The main criticism that can be levelled at some church prayer meetings is that they have become backward looking in the sense that those who attend do what has always been done at such meetings. The pattern is invariably the same. A regular number of hymns is chosen and they always fill the same slots. The minister speaks for half an hour, and he knows exactly how many sheets of notes he needs to fill the allotted time. He or some other respected leader announces a list of prayer topics and then (as if God had not heard the first time round) various members of the group use the topics as a basis for extemporary prayers. After one hour precisely, the meeting ends with 'the Grace' and those who have attended scatter to their homes, almost without speaking to each other, lest small talk should spoil the piety of the occasion.

That may sound like an unkind and perversely cynical assessment of sincere and well meant spiritual activity. But there must be some reason why so much effort is put in at such gatherings, with such small results. So few of our praying churches today grow with a crusading zeal that approximates, even to a small degree, to the life of the early church. Could it be that in many of our small group prayer times – even those attended by the keenest praying members of our churches – we are trapped into a habit of repeating what has been done in all our yesterdays, and actually fail to get in touch with our living, powerful, contemporary God *today*? And if we fail to make contact *today*, however can we know his will for *tomorrow*? It is too easy to get stuck even in godly ruts and to make gospel religion into an irrelevant ritual.

In being critical of this way of doing things at St John's, we were being critical of ourselves. Someone has said, 'The trouble with most of us is that we would rather be ruined by praise than saved by criticism.' Our self criticism was made in the presence of God, and led us to seek him in a more real way.

Features of the 'Open to God' groups

Our aim in meeting 'Open to God' style was to find a way of being as intimately in touch with God as the first Christians were. When the rulers, elders and teachers of the law hauled Peter and John before them, 'they saw the courage of Peter and John and realised that they were unschooled, ordinary men. They were astonished and they took note that these men had been with Jesus' (Acts 4:13). We looked for that kind of life-changing encounter with our living Lord. To achieve it the meeting had to be set up in a certain way, bearing in mind that it would comprise about twenty-four church members, who had pledged themselves to a specific 'togetherness' in seeking God and his will.

Firstly, the group met on church premises, so that nobody felt barred from it. For example, it was not the social custom in some parts of our parish for people to meet freely in other people's homes. With a congregation that was very mixed, socially, it was important not to allow a social factor to prevent us achieving a spiritual goal. The meeting could have been held in the vicarage, but that location had as much disadvantage as a home in a wealthy section of the parish. Both would have large enough rooms for such a meeting, but neither was neutral territory where any member of the congregation could participate freely. The point about the early disciples having 'everything in common' (Acts 2:44) was that there was total mutuality and sharing so that no one was left out for any social or material reason. So we met in one of the church rooms.

Secondly, the ordained staff did not dominate the meeting. The chairs were put out in a circle so that no individual sat in a place of leadership or headship. Equally, didactic studies were not prepared in advance even though on all other teaching occasions material was meticulously prepared and written out in full. We had to trust that God would speak to us through one another, and I had to learn not to panic about a meeting for which I felt responsible, but for which I had not prepared in the normal manner. Only with this degree of openness on the part of the leadership could the group truly be open to God, allowing him to speak through one and another in the course of the meeting.

Thirdly, we had to be open-ended in respect of timing. If we had all packed up our hymn books and Bibles after one hour, there would have been a built-in constraint in our gathering. In typical English style we should have got out our Filofaxes and said to God: 'Yes, we can spare you that one hour early on a Saturday morning, but after that we have many other things to see to.' If we had been too busy to pray longer and wait for God's breakthrough, we should have been too busy, full stop. In practice the meeting usually lasted between one and a half or two hours, but we were always ready to go on all day if God called us to.

Fourthly, the gathering was not merely pietistic and devotional. We were not coming together simply to find strength and mutual support in order to stagger on for another day or two with God, before the next church service or prayer meeting. Instead, all the practical issues of church life and witness were laid before those who assembled together. One week, for example, we were seeking God about evangelism. Another week we prayed about our social witness concerning pornography, as sex shops were opening up in Birmingham.

Prayer

With these guidelines the group developed such a sense of working together in God's presence, that there was a high degree of awareness of the times when God was speaking to us. We were of one mind about what we were called to do, and about how we were directed to pray. One example will serve to illustrate.

We had a problem in the life of the church because a number of people seemed to mis-hear either what was said from the pulpit or in the notices in church. On one occasion a student approached me after a sermon I had preached on the text, 'Jesus Christ is the same yesterday and today and for ever' (Hebrews 13:8). He said that he had disagreed with me when I said that God was changing in every generation, and that the God and Father we worship today is not the same as the God and Father of our Lord Jesus Christ. This was, of course, exactly the opposite of what I had said in the pulpit, but he made it clear to me that this key aspect of our church's ministry was under spiritual attack. I was reminded of the words of my predecessor, Canon Leathem, when he expressed his concern that so few had been converted at St John's over recent years, despite faithful gospel preaching. I wondered if it was because people had been mis-hearing sermons over the years. An obvious ploy of the evil one would be to confuse the minds of those hearing God's word so that they could not respond to the good news of Jesus.

We took the problem to the 'Open to God' meeting the next Saturday morning. Immediately one of the older women present recalled that she had had a similar experience with an elderly lady who was regularly attending spiritulist seances at the local school. 'The caretaker there is a leading healing medium,' we were informed. With this news, which came as a surprise to everyone present including the vicar, we all waited on God. Then one of our number spoke out. 'I believe we are called to bind Satan so that no one ever again mis-hears the word of God when it is preached in St John's.' Through another person we were assured that there would never again be a Guest Service at which people were specially invited to hear the gospel preached without conversions to Christ. Over eighteen years that promise has proved true.

We were able, similarly, to pray through other pastoral situations in the church. Although we were in one sense rather passively waiting on God, the prayer was leading to specific guidance about how to act in practical ways.

After three years, the freedom of the 'Open to God' style of meeting replaced the more formal pattern of the Tuesday night prayer meeting and it grew in leaps and bounds. From some twenty or so who met for prayer on Tuesdays the meeting suddenly became eighty-strong. Then it jumped to 120 and eventually some 300 were attending regularly and we had to move into the church itself.

Praise

When 'Open to God' took the place eventually of the old style church prayer meeting and grew in numbers by sudden and quite unexpected leaps and bounds, we found that our extended times of waiting on God had led to a quite new ability of holding together in times of corporate praise. Prior to that our tradition in the church prayer time had been one of dour, hard-working intercession. Of course, there are many New Testament instances of united prayer being crucial in the extension of God's work. We have seen one example in the prayer time following Peter and John's arrest. Another is described in Acts 12 when James had been killed and Peter imprisoned under the persecution of King Herod. We read that, as Peter was kept in prison, 'the church was earnestly praying to God for him' (Acts 12:5). In a moment of humour Luke records the surprise of those praying when Peter arrived at their meeting, with a testimony of angelic visitation, in order to get him out of gaol. As a fellowship we could identify with that sort of half-believing intercession – a meeting of solemn-faced Christians mouthing words which conform well to an idiom and style of Christian behavioural pattern, but which often lack deep conviction before God. Fortunately, his love and mercy is such that he gives gracious deliverance in answer to prayer even when we lack the faith to expect it.

The genuineness of the church's prayer for Peter is shown by the fact that it was a heart cry 'to God' (v 5). Similarly, in the earlier incident, the disciples began their prayer, 'Sovereign Lord, you made the heaven and the earth and the sea, and everything in them. You spoke by the Holy Spirit through the mouth of your servant, our father David' (Acts 4:24–25). At the heart of such God-centredness is praise to the God who has revealed his power and love in creation and history, and has spoken by his servants through centuries of time. Too often our intercession focuses on the *needs* and *ills* of the world and of our friends in the church. Somehow it is easier to describe Aunt Agatha's symptoms of arthritis in our prayers, than to focus our minds on God's greatness in creating and rescuing us.

We had to relearn how to pray, making the transition from heavy, works-based intercession where everything seemed to depend on us, to glad and liberated praise, where we looked for the grace of God to be released amongst us as we acknowledged his greatness. It took several months to make this change. To help us, the leader of the meeting would intervene if one of the group 'lowered the tone' from praise to intercession. As gently as possible, he would urge us to move back onto the 'wavelength' of praise and worship. 'Great is the Lord, and most worthy of praise' (Psalm 48:1), he would remind us. Soon the flow of unceasing praise could continue again: 'I will praise you, O Lord, with all my heart;' someone in the back row would proclaim, 'before the "gods" I will sing your praise' (Psalm 138:1). As people sat with Bibles open, the Psalms would frequently be the inspiration for our praise as our minds wandered through the Old Testament worship song book, that 'smouldering volcano of praise', as Professor James Stewart has described it.

It has to be said that this new lift of praise in the life of the group coincided with many people in the congregation experiencing a new depth of the Holy Spirit's working in their lives. For some this was a dramatic encounter with God which they described in terms of a fresh 'baptism of the Holy Spirit'. For others it was a gentle awakening to a new dimension of the Spirit's love and grace in their lives.

Perhaps this was the most significant result of the earlier times of waiting on God in the smaller group. Without any sense of demanding a specific sort of experience of the Spirit, evidenced by certain spiritual gifts, God moved in hundreds of lives. The congregation did not divide into 'haves' and 'have nots' in terms of spiritual experiences, but it was characterised by a new quality of praise and by a hunger for extended times of worship. We noted that many of the canticles we had long been accustomed to sing in our Anglican liturgical form of worship at Morning and Evening Prayer, were in fact songs given to the church when individuals were freshly filled with the Spirit (see Luke 1:46–55; 1:67–79; 2:27–32). We understood the praise of the first Christians after the Spirit had been poured out at Pentecost (Acts 2:42–47), and wondered at Stephen, the first martyr, looking up to heaven even while being stoned to death, seeing 'the glory of God, and Jesus standing at the right hand of God' (Acts 7:55). We rejoiced at the confidence of Paul and Silas incarcerated in a Philippian gaol and 'praying and singing hymns to God' at midnight (Acts 16:25).

Into small groups

For some years now this larger meeting has alternated with home group meetings on the same night of the week. Although more than 200 people attend regularly, it provides the opportunity for a 'togetherness' in praise and worship. The informal worship expressed then, with songs and choruses, balances the more formal worship of Sunday services. Elements of praise, intercessory prayer, testimony, shared scripture and expository teaching are always present, with the main emphasis being on an extended time of open worship.

We recognised, though, that more of the 'fringe' members of the congregation needed to be drawn into the reality of its fellowship and service. Many felt lost in the large Sunday worship times and with the midweek 'Open to God' meeting at the 200 mark, that wasn't much better! So we decided to divide the congregation into eight sub-churches, which we call Community Groups, and into a number of smaller Home Groups. Each Community Group unites three or four Home Groups under a leader distinct from the Home Group Leaders.

One week we meet in Home Groups and on alternate weeks we meet together as a large 'Open to God' group. On these occasions the congregation breaks into four Community Groups after an hour of worship and teaching. The Community Groups then focus primarily on the prayer needs of the church and provide an important time of communication for planning practical activities.

The aim of the Home Groups is to continue the pattern of praise, prayer, teaching and open worship established by the 'Open to God' group, but on a more intimate level. This makes possible the meeting of needs and the exercise of gifts often prevented by the dynamics of a larger group.

One difficulty we met with when the larger 'Open to God' meeting broke down into smaller Home Groups, was that it was less easy for small groups to sustain the element of praise. There was no less *desire* to praise God, simply a difficulty in making sure that all the groups had a sufficient strength of musical talent to lead the worship. However, the praise that was hard to express with smaller numbers in the intimacy of the home was stimulated by the larger meeting on alternate weeks.

By following the pattern we find both in the Gospels and the Acts of the Apostles – and having groups of varying sizes within the main congregation – we found that different needs could be met at different levels. The key thing has been for *each segment* of the congregation to maintain *all the elements* of the life of the whole church: togetherness in prayer, study, fellowship, praise, worship, evangelism and pastoral care, and to be willing to be flexible enough to change the patterns as the changing needs of the congregation may require.

2
The value
of
small groups

In an essay titled, 'The Twelve Men', G K Chesterton wrote, 'Whenever our civilisation wants a library to be catalogued, or a solar system discovered, or any other trifle of this kind, it uses up its specialists. But when it wishes anything done which is really serious, it collects twelve of the ordinary men standing around. The same thing was done, if I remember right, by the Founder of Christianity.'

The small group of men gathered around Jesus was fundamental to the founding of the church and the establishing of the Kingdom of God on earth. Their togetherness began with a simple call, 'Come, follow me' (Matthew 4:19) and it was this command that brought them into a relationship with the Master and also into a new spiritual relationship with each other. So important was the choice of this first Christian group that Jesus spent the night in prayer before calling the disciples into special friendship. Then 'he called his disciples to him and chose twelve of them' (Luke 6:13). Jesus himself was the source of their unity and agreement, since there could hardly be a more diverse group of people. In normal human society, like-minded people tend to group together around a common interest. It might be madrigal singing, beer drinking, a sporting activity or adult education classes. Social factors of class, money and available facilities, draw together people with particular gifts and interests. A Christian group is different. It is not like a club to which people belong for pleasure or convenience. The uniting factor is Jesus, his love and the possession of his Spirit. He brings together the fishermen, the zealot and the tax collector. He joins the Sons of Thunder, the arch-pessimist and the traitor in bonds of friendship.

But companionship with Christ and with each other was not the only reason for being together.

Learning

The first followers were not just the precursors of kingdom relationships, nor were they simply living illustrations of new standards of love and mutual acceptance in the family of God. By definition, the disciples were *learners* in the school of Christ. They were apprentices, learning on the job from the teaching and example of their master craftsman. The idea of apprenticeship is peculiarly appropriate since the first followers of Jesus were quite young men. James Stewart points this out: 'Christianity began as a young people's movement. In thinking of Jesus and his disciples that is the first fact to make clear. Unfortunately it is a fact which Christian art and Christian preaching have too often obscured. But it is quite certain that the original disciple band was a young men's group. Most of the disciples were probably still in their twenties when they went out after Jesus.' (*The Life and Teaching of Jesus Christ*, J S Stewart. London: SCM Press, p 61.)

Because of the emphasis on adult small groups in the church today, it is often forgotten that the young people's Bible Class has a long and honourable history. Many church leaders found their early inspiration either in church-based or interdenominational Bible Class movements. The small group network in any local church must not neglect those groups which consist mainly of young people and their leaders. In the first parish in which I served, St Paul's, Woking, many of the young people who first responded to the call of Christ had no background of churchgoing. Nor were they 'bookish', in the sense that it was natural for them to be in a group with Bibles open, sharing the teaching of Christ. At first their concentration span was four minutes, so the Bible teaching slot never exceeded that time. However, as they grew in discipleship their hunger for the Bible grew and, within a very few months, it was possible to relate Bible study to set books in their RE examinations at school. Their Christian lives blossomed in the small group situation, and in time their eager witness to schoolfriends transformed the meeting into a large group.

Jesus taught as much as he could to the twelve in the short time available to him. That must be our ambition too. The world can entertain and amuse far better than we can within the limitations of our church premises or our homes. The one distinctive thing we can offer as Christians is the teaching of Jesus. He said, 'Come to me . . . learn from me' (Matthew 11:28–29). And his purpose was that they in turn should teach others. Jesus called them to 'be with him . . . that he might send them out to preach' (Mark 3:14). They were to evangelise, communicate and inform others about the kingdom of God – all part of a teaching task.

In the apprenticeship Jesus offered, he taught by example, in the miracles he performed and in the love he expressed to needy and lonely individuals in the crowds who followed. But he taught more directly too; all his words had a teaching purpose. Not everyone found his teaching easy to accept. 'On hearing it, many of his disciples said, "This is a hard teaching. Who can accept it?" ' (John 6:60.) His teaching in the temple courts about his divine origin and unique relationship with the Father angered his opponents: ' "I am not here on my own, but he who sent me is true. You do not know him, but I know him because I am from him and he sent me." At this they tried to seize him.' (John 7:28–30.) However, those with faith said, with Nicodemus, 'Rabbi, we know you are a teacher who has come from God' (John 3:2).

Today there are many people who are not committed followers of Jesus but are prepared to acknowledge him as a great teacher, and who note the impact of his teaching on the world. The historian, Kenneth Scott Latourette, commenting on the world-changing effect of Jesus' teaching, writes: 'As the centuries pass, the evidence accumulating by his effect on history is that Jesus' life is the most influential life ever lived on this planet. That influence appears to be mounting.' It is because the words of Jesus were never purely local or temporal in their application that we must heed them as urgently as those first disciples did during their apprenticeship with Jesus. The small group that meets for prayer, worship, testimony and Bible Study may seem startlingly irrelevant to the headline affairs of the world's press, but if Jesus' teaching is at the heart of it, that group will be an essential unit for each member's growth in godliness, without which none of us will influence any headlines at all, whether national or local.

Jesus' use of the small group for teaching sets the pattern for us. Within this overall structure, we can note two more things. Firstly, Jesus taught with *authority*. His teaching was different in quality from that of the religious leaders of his day: 'The people were amazed at his teaching, because he taught as one who had authority, not as the teachers of the law' (Mark 1:22). The teachers of the law would 'compare and contrast' the teaching of the scholars, and to come to tentative and arguable conclusions. Jesus' words rang out with God's own unmistakable authority. Students know how some writers have a gift of teaching that sets out their thinking so simply, while at the same time being deeply profound. Jesus had this quality to the highest degree, so that those who heard him did not have to debate or interpret his meaning. His message was clear and it came with authority.

In home group discussions it is easy to impose our own interpretation on a Bible passage and give vent to our pet theories. If we do that we are no better than the teachers of the law. We must allow God's own teaching to break through to our minds, so that we are then moved to obedience. The authority of Jesus must still prevail, so that the teaching and learning experience of the group is much more than the sharing of human, bright ideas. The group should not offer second-hand religion, but the authoritative teaching of Jesus. This can only happen if Bible studies are adequately prepared by the leader and, ideally, by other group members too. Then scripture can be compared with scripture, just as Jesus used Old Testament scripture and applied it to his contemporary situation.

Secondly, his teaching was *authoritative* because he set up himself as the example the disciples were to follow. When Alan Stibbs lectured on the Gospels at Oak Hill College he brought the opening chapters of Mark's Gospel vividly to life, by showing how every event in the ministry of Jesus was a practical lesson for the followers in his training school. They were learning on the job as Jesus showed them *how* to minister. He was, by every powerful action, teaching *who* he was. He is the one who delivers us from the power of evil, who heals our sicknesses, calms our storms and transforms our lives.

In the small group what we learn about Jesus should be translated into *active response* to him. This will happen as we allow him to minister to us through the others present, and give ourselves to them in the same way.

Worship

Those of Jesus' followers who had 'ears to hear' recognised that they were privileged to walk with the Son of God on earth. John the Baptist recognised it immediately. He gave his testimony of what he had seen at Jesus' baptism: 'I saw the Spirit come down from heaven as a dove and remain on him. I would not have known him, except that the one who sent me to baptise with water told me, "The man on whom you see the Spirit come down and remain is he who will baptise with the Holy Spirit." I have seen and I testify that this is the Son of God' (John 1:32–34). Later, Jesus' confident declaration of forgiveness to the paralysed man caused even his religious enemies to recognise that he was claiming to be God on earth (Luke 5:17–26). And he spelt out to them plainly, 'You are from below; I am from above. You are of this world; I am not of this world' (John 8:23).

The presence of the 'other-worldly' Son of God among his small group of friends, brought a new dynamic to worship. The first disciples found that being in conversational closeness with the Son of God meant a completely new experience of worship. It was so different from worshipping God in the formal style of organised worship occasions. In one sense worship is a concept to be argued about. We all like different styles of worship; we are all influenced by the different traditions in which we grew up. We have views about the content of the services, the balance between noise and silence, activity and contemplation, old language or new, hymns or choruses, liturgy or spontaneous contributions. When we argue about the 'how' of worship, we tend to get stuck there with our prejudices. The woman whom Jesus met at the well did just that. In order to help her respond to all that he had to offer her as God's Messiah Jesus knew he had to touch directly on her sinful relationships and immoral lifestyle. But such close confrontation was too uncomfortable for her. She immediately tried to turn his attention away from her personal life, to the more theological issue of worship. ' "Sir," the woman said, "I can see that you are a prophet. Our fathers worshipped on this mountain, but you Jews claim that the place where we must worship is in Jerusalem." ' (John 4:19–20.) She saw worship in terms of human traditions and customs. But Jesus focused her attention onto God himself: 'a time is coming and has now come when the true worshippers will worship the Father in spirit and in truth, for they are the kind of worshippers the Father seeks' (John 4:23).

Because of the appearance of Jesus on earth, everything is different. The old disputes no longer count. His presence with us brings the King to his kingdom, and the presence of God into our worship. This woman soon forgot her smoke-screen questions and began to worship Jesus himself as Messiah. Soon 'many of the Samaritans from that town believed in him because of the woman's testimony' (John 4:39).

The Father still 'seeks' worshippers – those who will worship the Jesus way, 'in spirit and in truth.' This is where the worship of a small group of Christians can be like that of the disciples, as they experienced the companionship of Jesus. Of course, there were occasions when large crowds heard his teaching, as in the Sermon on the Mount. But the Gospel story is about learning to live in close proximity with God. The tension of acknowledging the glory of God in his transcendence and of discovering the love and acceptance of God in his immanence has always been there.

It is the tension of learning to honour God while living intimately with him. The pattern Jesus laid down – that of living with a group of disciples who love him and reverence him – is a sure guide for what a home group should be. Without the splendour of a specialist church building, God is real by his Spirit in some-one's front room, when a group of believing disciples worship him there together.

The practicalities of doing this are outlined elsewhere in this book. The small group of ordinary Christians in a church group may lack experienced worship leadership or be short of musicians. But, where God is present, worship is called out of us. In the small, informal setting we might not use the words of liturgical statement and response: 'The Lord is here; his Spirit is with us,' but each person attending the meeting is aware that the Lord really is with them. We should not allow ourselves to be discouraged by a lack of human resource, when all we need is God-centred faith and a willingness to open our hearts to him.

Fellowship

Commitment to one another
The small group offers the ideal opportunity for members of a church to progress beyond the 'hello' relationships of superficial contact at the church door, to deep relationships within which Christians take serious responsibility for each other. Just as an orchestra is free to be a vehicle for beautiful music only when the members are committed to each other – to learn and rehearse together, to feel for each other and become sensitive to each other's gifts and talents – so the small group can only operate as a unit when there is a commitment which goes beyond a mouth-ing of surface greetings or even of 'spiritual' talk. Fellowship speaks of mutual sharing; partnership that involves giving, serv-ing, caring and working together. Basic to it is the sort of unity and togetherness we have already looked at. Paul said, 'If you have any encouragement from being united with Christ, if any comfort from his love, if any fellowship with the Spirit, if any tenderness and compassion, then make my joy complete by being

like-minded, having the same love, being one in spirit and purpose. Do nothing out of selfish ambition or vain conceit, but in humility consider others better than yourselves' (Philippians 2:1–3). The way for 'Jesus life' to be lived out in our world is for communities to build themselves on these qualities.

Often, it is selfishness rather than selflessness, that prevails in the small group setting. Each member can be more concerned to 'get something out of' the group than to express 'tenderness and compassion' for those others in it. Alternatively, group members may feel threatened and exposed by insensitive or overbearing leadership rather than gaining 'encouragement' and 'comfort'. One person feels threatened at not knowing Bible texts and references, another is afraid to pray aloud. Another shows her insecurity by laying on a vast spread at the refreshment time, to outdo others and say, in effect, 'well, I may be no good at the spiritual side of things, but at least I can cook better than last week's hostess!' Subtly, our pride and fears prevail and, in different ways, we try to outdo one another instead of counting others better than ourselves. Paul's recipe for fellowship is this: 'Each of you should look not only to your own interests, but also to the interests of others. Your attitude should be the same as that of Christ Jesus' (Philippians 2:4–5). Paul then goes on to give us a moving description of the self-humbling of Jesus, to make sure that we have the right model in front of us for fellowship with one another.

Although the crucial factor for such Christian fellowship to be expressed is that each one should already have 'fellowship with the Spirit', the small group leader has a great responsibility for encouraging and developing right attitudes. She can put forward schemes for developing the art of giving and sharing. She can spot needs in the wider church life that the members of the group can meet together. She can organise outings and fellowship meals, encouraging joint meetings with other groups at a social level or for shared communion services or agape meals.

A fellowship of the 'unlike'
There is a tendency for some small groups to choose members who are naturally like-minded and share similar human interests.

The whole point of 'fellowship in the Spirit' is that in Christ, through the Spirit, there is a gift of shared life which *totally transforms and transcends* normal human relationships. The old chorus spells out the new togetherness:

'Red and yellow, black and white
All are precious in his sight
Jesus died for all the children of the world.'

My travels abroad have emphasised this for me. Whether one is ministering in the simple brick and wood, open-sided hall in the backyard of a Peruvian shanty town, or in the corrugated iron church of the township of Alexandria in Johannesburg: sharing with Christians in a black Pentecostal church in Birmingham, or in the middle of a civil war in Nigeria, ministering to students who are the solitary survivors out of their families, there is instant, unassailable, total oneness which breaks down all differences of suffering, deprivation, class, privilege, language or colour. There is the peace Jesus alone can give (John 14:27). It is a peace of relationships, a harmony of spirit, a mutual respecting and knowing, which shames the world's differences and divisions and demonstrates the unique fellowship that Christians are called to enjoy.

It is therefore inexcusable for groups to be exclusive so that only like-minded people of similar interests and similar standing in society come together. The mistake that many churches have made over a long period of time has been to encourage fellowship on the basis of church organisations – Women's Fellowship, Young Wives, Men's Groups, and so on. This limits, by definition, the sort of person who can attend. It divides families and divides the church into segments of life spiralling off after their own separate interests and different programmes. By contrast, a network of small groups, centred on Christ, aiming to live out 'fellowship with the Spirit' and making 'every effort to keep the unity of the Spirit through the bond of peace' (Ephesians 4:3), transcends all such divisions. The resultant variety of people within each group can then be a living illustration that, 'There is one body and one Spirit – just as you were called to one hope when you were called – one Lord, one faith, one baptism; one

God and Father of all, who is over all and through all and in all' (Ephesians 4:4–6). The unity of diverse people reveals the unity of the Godhead to the world. So we dare exclude no one. If Christian faith shared in the wider world can transcend deep human divisions, it must be seen to do so in the fellowship of the local church too, and it is the task of leadership to make sure it does.

The leader's role

How can this unity be achieved? Here are some of the basic issues to consider.

First, the leader needs to be sensitive to the social and intellectual differences among group members. The person who likes to show how much he knows must not be allowed to dominate the conversation. The leader may need to have a private, corrective word with him. If the meeting becomes too bookish or cerebral for some, it is the leader's responsibility to lighten the tone and make the focal point more practical. If a shy or less confident person plucks up courage to ask a question, it might be helpful for the leader to let the theme of the meeting be diverted in order to deal with that question, rather than continue slavishly with the published subject. When I was responsible for a mixed group of young believers in a parish in Woking, I would frequently change the thrust of a Bible study if one of them brought an unbelieving friend to the meeting. The key is that the whole group is, at the leader's discretion, willing to surrender itself to the needs of just one of its members – the newcomer for instance – and to trust the leader to make the subject matter relevant to them all.

Secondly, personality clashes and disharmony can occur within the group. In such cases I advise leaders to suggest that those in conflict resolve their dispute by the pattern Jesus outlined in Matthew 18. First, the aggrieved party should go to his brother or sister in Christ and explain what's hurt or upset him. If his approach falls on deaf ears he should then take 'one or two others along, so that "every matter may be established by the testimony of two or three witnesses." If he refuses to listen to them, tell it to the church . . .' (Matthew 18:15–17). When the group leader challenges those who sin against each other to be as open as this, the argument is often easily resolved. It is more difficult if the leader is the one at fault, or the one who feels sinned against. In such a case, the wider eldership of the church may be needed to heal the dispute. The words of Jesus are strong against the offender who will not listen to the judgement of the church: 'If he refuses to listen even to the church, treat him as you would a pagan or a tax collector' (Matthew 18:17).

In the church today we often lack this sense of discipline and good order in relationships. But if we are to witness to the love and unity we have in Christian fellowship, there must be a way of resolving conflict. The world does it by walk-outs and resignations. We cannot resign from being brothers and sisters in God's family, and the more we work in close contact with each other in small groups, the more risk there is that, as brothers and sisters fall out with each other in human families, so we may in the church family. As the principles taught by Jesus in Matthew 18 are applied by the group leader, the small group should grow into a caring and considerate community that actively *draws* people of varied backgrounds and abilities together and enables them to find a way of peace at any point of conflict and disagreement.

In Christ the deepest divisions of the world have been broken down: 'There is neither Jew nor Greek, slave nor free, male nor female, for you are all one in Christ Jesus' (Galatians 3:28). The aim of the small group should be to present the miracle of this sort of unity to a divided world. The sin of exclusiveness in the small group is that it bars others from sharing the life that God has given. People who may not yet be in a position to share the life of the group will be made aware of its special quality of Christ-centred life, through the evidence of the changed, enriched lives of those who belong to and benefit from the group. So the aim of the leader in pastoral care and in developing fellowship is not just to help individuals at their point of need but to have a vision of what a renewed community might become, by God's grace, and then to lead in such a way that everything is done to bring that vision into reality.

A renewed community must be characterised by loving

relationships, and at home group level it is likely to have the natural family as its model. Human parents represent God's fatherhood on earth, and direct their family's life so that it is a place where children learn how to relate to each other, the Lord, and the wider world. In the same way, the small group leader has a 'parental' role of oversight and direction. He has the right to say, 'we don't behave like that here, because we are a Christian family group, and we must live up to the standards of our Father.' With these boundaries, as the group interacts in social as well as spiritual activities, it becomes a microcosm of heavenly realities and relationships. The love its members discover together should then spread into the wider life of the church.

Evangelism

The small group learning, worshipping and sharing fellowship together must become the small group witnessing together. The tasks go hand in hand and it is our call to proclaim Christ in his fullness that should sharpen our minds as we study and pray together.

The early church

The early church grew because the first groups of Christians were never content to remain inward looking. In the early days the groups were always small enough to meet in homes. We read that, 'they broke bread in their homes and ate together with glad and sincere hearts, praising God and enjoying the favour of all the people. And the Lord added to their number daily those who were being saved' (Acts 2:46–47). God did not work through huge congregations of believers with powerful preachers trained in homiletics. There were none. The church was simply a collection of small, home-based groups, praying, praising and learning together, but also being powerfully effective in outreach and evangelism. After Peter's first Spirit-filled sermon on the day of Pentecost 'about three thousand were added to their number' (Acts 2:41).

Here was a church which took seriously the final commission

of Jesus. He had said, 'All authority in heaven and on earth has been given to me. Therefore go and make disciples of all nations, baptising them in the name of the Father and of the Son and of the Holy Spirit, and teaching them to obey everything I have commanded you. And surely I will be with you always, to the very end of the age' (Matthew 28:18–20). The first Christians lived as though there was no other task to be done but to win the world for their Master. They were described as those 'who turned the world upside down' (Acts 17:6, *RSV*). Before long the church was tested by severe persecution and 'all except the apostles were scattered throughout Judea and Samaria' (Acts 8:1). But even without apostolic example and leadership, 'those who had been scattered abroad preached the word wherever they went' (Acts 8:4). Philip, the deacon, took on an apostolic role of church planting in an evangelistic outreach into Samaria, accompanied by signs and wonders. 'When the crowds heard Philip and saw the miraculous signs he did, they all paid close attention to what he said. With shrieks, evil spirits came out of many, and many paralytics and cripples were healed. So there was great joy in that city' (Acts 8:6–7).

As the church's witness spread from Jerusalem to Judea, Samaria and then 'to the ends of the earth,' the small, seeking, praying group was still the key factor in the church's advance. Indeed it could be said that the gospel spread into the whole of western civilisation because Paul and Silas attended a small gathering of women who met for prayer at Philippi: 'On the Sabbath we went outside the city gate to the river, where we expected to find a place of prayer. We sat down and began to speak to the women who had gathered there' (Acts 16:13). A key convert on that occasion was Lydia, a middle-aged businesswoman who travelled the trade routes selling purple cloth. From that small prayer group a notable evangelist emerged to further the work of the gospel.

Similarly, at Ephesus Paul started off by teaching a group of about twelve disciples who were confused about baptism and what was involved in a genuine experience of the Holy Spirit in their lives. This small group then formed the basis of a thriving church (Acts 19:1–7).

The image: big = successful

Today we suffer from the handicap of a glorious past. We see the testimony to it in the large number of huge Victorian churches which have either been converted so that smaller congregations can worship without discomfort or have been sold off. Older Christians remember the days when churches were packed with worshippers; today that is the exception rather than the rule. Equally, the image society had of its church in the past is very different from that held today. I once met a lady who, as a small child, walked many miles with her family to hear the great Charles Spurgeon preach at the Metropolitan Chapel at the Elephant and Castle in South London. In those days it seemed that people went 'to hear the preacher', who was a star figure in society. All the large centres of population had their noted preacher. Today the memory of them remains in faded photographs on vestry walls; austere, authoritative figures to whom the multitudes listened in rapt attention.

In contrast to those days of numerical success, the church in Great Britain has tended to present a picture of failure and decline. Between the mid 1970s and the mid 1980s the churches in England lost over half a million members (*UK Christian Handbook* 1985/6. Bromley: Marc Europe, p 107). Aware of the church's current weakness we tend to equate small numbers with failure. The New Testament, by contrast, presents small groups as springboards for invading the culture of society around, a culture often dominated by the worship of other gods. Paul saw the group of twelve at Ephesus as the start of something new, big and exciting, the means for winning new disciples to Christ.

Catching the vision

In our Church's life we have not found it easy to convey this vision of witness and evangelism to our small home groups. There have been a few notable exceptions, but these have been groups which were inaugurated with a specifically evangelistic aim. The leader taught the group members how to win people for Christ, how to use the Bible in argument and debate, and suggested methods for reaching their neighbourhood with the gospel. They visited door to door, invited friends to evangelistic services in church, held open meetings in their homes at which a visiting evangelist spoke and, most successfully of all, the wives held coffee mornings to which they invited friends to hear the gospel explained. However, this vision has never been caught on a wide scale since most groups seem content to maintain their meetings as times of fellowship, prayer and Bible study. The group ends up meeting the needs of its members rather than reaching out to the needs of a godless neighbourhood.

From time to time we assess our impact on the world around us by asking the congregation how many friends they have outside the life of the church. If all our time is spent socialising with Christians or attending meetings at church, we have no hope at all of penetrating the wider society with the gospel. On occasions we even lay aside an evening when we would normally meet in home groups so that the whole congregation can pledge to invite people into their homes for a meal, in order to further friendship with those outside the church. Learning from Billy Graham's 1986 *Mission England* campaign we encourage even smaller groupings of prayer triplets in our ongoing programme of evangelism.

Small-group support for evangelism

However, the primary evangelistic work of the small groups in our church is in their prayer back-up for well organised programmes of every-member evangelism, undertaken as the responsibility of the whole church. The problem in many churches is that the evangelistic task is always left to a few enthusiasts. These few become a pressure group, cajoling others into action, often feeling unsupported by the bulk of church members. They become overworked, dispirited and thoroughly disillusioned. Others in the church resent their criticism and rightly feel that not every Christian is gifted or called to be an evangelist.

We set about solving this problem by seeking God's answer in the original, small 'Open to God' group. Our questions were, 'What do we do, Lord, about the apathy and lack of concern for evangelism? How do we organise ourselves to have far greater evangelistic impact than we do at the moment?'

The answer given through one of our members to the first

question was that we should pray that people who lived in our area should become more and more miserable! This shocked us at first, until we realised that it was not an unkind prayer. Rather, it was asking that those who were unaware of being sinners in God's sight should be helped to a conviction of sin by the Holy Spirit, and then, from an awareness of their miserable condition without Christ, might turn to him for forgiveness. There was a direct answer to that prayer for those on our evangelistic visiting team. Two of our burly male visitors knocked on a front door towards the end of an evening's work. It was past 9 pm – hardly the time to receive callers in an area of the city where muggings and even murder is not unknown. The door was opened by an older lady who had been forewarned of the possibility of such a call that evening by a letter from the vicar. Such letters had been delivered during the previous week to each home in the area we planned to visit. 'Come in,' she said, 'I'm so glad you've come. For some reason I've been getting more and more miserable recently, and I'm sure you have the answer to my problem!' She, of course, had no way of knowing the terms of our prayer for her neighbourhood, but her ready response gave our visitors an immediate opening to speak of their faith in Christ.

We had a similar direct answer to our prayer about the impact of our Sunday evangelistic services. Again, through one of those present at the 'Open to God' meetings, God told us to pray that before a word was spoken or a hymn was sung at an evangelistic service, people arriving in church would be overwhelmed with a tremendous sense of the Lord's presence and power. Since then, time and again when newly converted people have given their testimony, they have said that they were 'overwhelmed with a tremendous sense of God's presence and power' as they sat in church before the service began. Similarly, none of those giving testimony knew anything of the wording of our prayers behind the scenes.

In this way the prayer backing and discernment of Christians in the smaller groups has ongoing, vital impact on the evangelism of the whole fellowship.

In fact, the whole evangelistic project in the parish of St John's stemmed from a clear directive from God in the 'Open to God' setting. We wondered how to counter the disappointment of those two or three enthusiasts for evangelism who shamed the inaction of the rest of the church. As we discussed the matter before God, we realised that the church had become a holy ghetto, totally out of touch with the 'good-natured pagans' who lived in most of the homes in our parish. When the question was asked, only one member of the congregation claimed to be in touch with unbelieving friends. However, we realised that it wasn't simply a matter of not sharing our faith with outsiders; few of us spoke of spiritual matters even to each other. This was the stimulus to divide our larger meetings up into a dozen or more small home groups. The aim was not just to have fellowship meetings, but to share Jesus with each other, in training for determined, outgoing evangelism which was planned to start some six months later. All members of the home groups were challenged to be the evangelists and some responded. The remainder turned their small group into a missionary prayer meeting. Others were enrolled to produce a 'Vicar's letter' personally addressed to the occupants of each home in the area to be visited. Yet others delivered copies of the letter door-to-door, so that everyone was properly warned of the prospective visit and invited to write to the vicarage declining a visit if they should wish to do so. A team of prayer partners was also established and arrangements were made for members of the evangelistic team to visit some of the afternoon home groups, largely attended by the elderly, in order to involve them in the project too. Others in the church were asked to babysit for team members and some offered their homes to be bases for the team when it was operating in their area of the parish.

In this way, every member ministry was expressed. Everybody in the church could have a part to play either in direct witness, believing prayer or practical, caring actions. The 'evangelists' were not an élite, specialist group, nor was there pressure on those not gifted to offer themselves for front-line evangelism. Since the visitors were sent out in pairs, there was an opportunity to put a more experienced Christian with the person who was going out for the first time. Furthermore, each team member was supported by the fellowship and prayer of a small home group.

The final important factor to record was that the parish was divided into six areas geographically, so that only one sixth was visited each year, once before Christmas and once after Christmas. This meant that each year's target was always attained – good for everyone's morale – and no individual became so overburdened with the evangelistic task that they could not keep up regular attendance at their small home group or the larger 'Open to God' gathering. Those who were giving out in witness and evangelism still had time to take in, in teaching, prayer, fellowship and worship, as well as having time for their own family life at home.

So, although it has not been easy to stimulate particular home groups to engage in direct evangelism, the group network is fundamental to the evangelistic task of the church as a whole.

Pastoral care

As well as providing the structure for evangelism, which can be shared in different ways by every church member, small groups enable a wide sharing in pastoral care. Unfortunately, as churches move away from New Testament patterns of ministry, they lose the vision of caring, person-to-person ministry in the church. There are congregations where 'ministry' at a personal level is not even looked for from the minister! The stiff upper lip characteristic of the British temperament causes many church members to suffer in silence, rather than open up their need for ministry and prayer. In church, people still expect to be preached at (though not for too long!), but they do not expect to be counselled in the study. If such personal ministry is to be achieved it has to stem from pastoral visiting in the home where the minister takes initiatives, drops hints and steers conversation as he senses some area of need that has to be opened up. All this happens within the context of the person's expectation of a polite afternoon tea call accompanied by inconsequential chat.

In some other congregations the desire for ministry has gone to the other extreme. Every church member expects access to the minister for regular counselling sessions and the measure of his success is marked by the fullness of his diary or appointment book. It would seem that the Christian life cannot be lived without the permanent support of a personal counsellor. Such an attitude denies the reality of the ongoing care, encouragement and working of God's Holy Spirit in the life of a Christian. Furthermore, it debases the value of the teaching sermon which, among other things, should be the vehicle for conveying the truths that many people insist on hearing face to face from their personal counsellor.

There is of course, a right balance. At times of crisis anyone should be willing to be open to receive counsel and care from the pastor or from another member of the church. At times of normal growth in the Christian life all the means of grace – preaching, fellowship, prayer, the sacraments – should encourage the Christian in his walk with God.

If church members have little desire to receive pastoral care from the minister of the church, they will have even less desire to receive it from the leader of a small home group. Equally, if the minister is overwhelmed by too great a demand for his counselling services, the small group leader who assumes a pastoral counselling role could also become totally consumed by the needs of the group. The answer is to put the emphasis on the *sharing of ministry* in the small group. This can be done by appointing more than one set of leaders in the group. Often a couple (either a married couple of a pair of single people) will assume the main responsibility of leadership, but another couple can serve alongside them, covering for absence, sharing hospitality and generally working together for the group's well-being and success.

Such a scheme encourages the possibility of multiplying the group when it becomes too large, since there is a built-in confidence in the deputy leadership. Incidentally, it is not always easy to form two new groups by dividing the old one into two exact halves. It works very much better for the original deputies or leader to move on to form a new group, perhaps taking just one or two with them. This becomes a mini church-planting situation, the new leaders drawing new disciples to themselves until a full-sized group is formed.

As members are encouraged to minister to each other, they become a source of mutual support in such a way that those who previously could not survive without permanent counsel and one-to-one care, find that they manage perfectly well. They discover an intimate sense of care in the small group and learn to trust God's love more fully in their daily lives. However, group leaders do need to develop some ability in pastoral care and counselling and also need to establish ways of protecting themselves from those who might demand too much of them. What we have found is that when many members of a large congregation belong to small groups, the pressure on the clergy largely disappears, and many of those who were previously well known for constantly seeking pastoral counsel, actually become those who share in the care of others. This is just what Paul expected to happen in the Corinthian church when he spoke of 'the God of all comfort, who comforts us in all our troubles, so that we can comfort those in any trouble with the comfort we ourselves have received from God' (2 Corinthians 1:3–4).

Training

For this to work out in practice, the group leader must see his task not just in terms of planning programmes, leading Bible studies or organising worship times or home group outings. Before accepting the task of leadership, the task of pastoral care should be recognised, some basic training given, and the cost of caring should be willingly accepted. It is possible to offer a fairly minimal standard of training through meetings for home group leaders and by occasional courses in pastoral counselling which the small group leaders are free to attend. Some leaders may attend specialist courses run by other Christian organisations, often on a national or regional basis, and others take up correspondence courses in pastoral care.

Paul himself gave this sort of instruction. It is fascinating to have his address to the Ephesian elders in Acts 20, since this is the only teaching in the whole of the Acts of the Apostles which is given to Christians rather than to those outside the church. Having reminded the elders of his own example in constant preaching, teaching and testifying to the gospel of Christ, he expressed afresh his commitment to the task to which they were called: 'I consider my life worth nothing to me, if only I may finish the race and complete the task the Lord Jesus has given me – the task of testifying to the gospel of God's grace' (Acts 20:24). Then he outlined their duties in pastoral care. Firstly, care of themselves, so that their own lives remained up to standard. Secondly, care for the people committed to their charge, working like a shepherd caring for his sheep: 'keep watch over yourselves and all the flock of which the Holy Spirit has made you overseers. Be shepherds of the church of God, which he bought with his own blood' (Acts 20:28).

Here we have an early use of the word *episkopos*, subsequently translated 'bishop'. In the modern church it has become confused with overtones of rank and seniority. Here in the *NIV* it is translated 'overseer' and simply meant 'shepherdly oversight' as Jesus expressed it in his own ministry – as the Good Shepherd who was willing to lay down his life for the sheep (John 10:11). The shepherd guarded, kept, fed and cared for the sheep, and a leader who follows Christ's example is committed to doing the same. And notice, Paul warns against possessiveness. A pastor can never refer to 'my group' or 'my church' because the flock has been purchased by God at the price of Christ's blood and it belongs only to him. Only the Holy Spirit appoints to the task of oversight, and our ministry can only succeed at his appointment. This is true at every level of serving God. When the deacons were appointed to free the apostles from having to 'wait on tables' (Acts 6:2), and to take over the practical task of sorting out the needs of the widows in the church, they chose men 'full of the Spirit and wisdom' (Acts 6:3). When we need group leaders in the church we do well not to call for volunteers but to seek those who are qualified for the task by the Spirit of God.

'Wolves'!

Paul continued the shepherding imagery in his charge to the Ephesian elders by warning of wolves who were likely to try and destroy the flock. These are enemies who come from outside the church to cause disruption and trouble. Often we are quick to welcome newcomers and slow to discern their true intent. Our own fellowship and one of our small home groups in particular were torn apart by the arrival in our midst of a woman who claimed gifts of ministry and insight from God. She was accepted lovingly by many of our people, and only when her behaviour was manifestly disruptive did we make investigation into her past. It turned out that in more than one notable church she had caused similar trouble and destroyed the faith of many. In the end, in an incident which hit the headlines of the national press, she was dismissed from her secular post. Then after many attempts at reconciliation in our fellowship, she had to be publicly dismissed from the church. Wolves are dangerous!

But so too are committed members of our own fellowship who for selfish reasons create rifts in the congregation: 'Even from among your own number men will arise and distort the truth in order to draw away disciples after them' (Acts 20:30). Many see a small group network in a church as a source of potential trouble. The fear is that some leaders might use their position to push their own views and to create a faction in the church. Recent church history is scattered with instances of lay leaders becoming impatient with the overall leadership of a church, and taking their group off to form a separate church in the neighbourhood. This is the risk of sharing ministry in small groups. It only works if there is an intense loyalty to the overall leadership of the church of which the groups are part. Usually the split happens because of pride and impatience. The small group leader wants to be Number One, not part of the team of ministers. Also, he often wants more excitement and more outward evidence of God's working, more quickly. It is sometimes possible by whipping up zeal and enthusiasm in a carnal way, to seem to produce this in the smaller group. Like-minded malcontents are drawn into the gathering from the main congregation, and sometimes from nearby churches too. But the person who is willing to head up such a rival faction is in grave danger of falling into the error that Paul warns against, of 'drawing away disciples'.

Sometimes the grievance is not so much about the style of worship, but the content of teaching. There are those in the church who sit under a well-prepared, well-thought-out, teaching sermon, eaten up with criticism in their hearts because the words are not phrased with a particular school of theological thought in mind, or the style does not match up in terms of content or delivery to that of some great master of the pulpit. On one occasion we had a small group who pulled away to set up a rival meeting at the same time as our co-ordinated system of small groups, because one man had backslidden from the fellowship and decided that the teaching was insufficiently Calvinistic. In counter-balancing what he conceived to be a false trend, he fell into deeper falsehood himself and in attempting to follow the great Reformer, John Calvin, taught a form of hyper-Calvinism which generously 'distorted the truth' as he drew certain disciples 'after him'. Sadly the group did not last long, since to our very great sorrow our brother left the church, though none of his followers went with him. He tried to establish his own church in another place, but it never grew.

For Paul this risk of defection was an urgent matter. He says, 'Be on your guard! Remember that for three years I never stopped warning each of you night and day with tears' (Acts 20:31). It was intolerable, in his view, to take any action which split apart the body of Christ. He appealed to the Christians at Corinth: 'I appeal to you, brothers, in the name of our Lord Jesus Christ, that all of you agree with one another so that there may be no divisions among you and that you may be perfectly united in mind and thought' (1 Corinthians 1:10). It was offensive to him that one should say, 'I follow Paul'; another, 'I follow Apollos'; another, 'I follow Cephas'; still another, 'I follow Christ' (1 Corinthians 1:12). This was the sort of division he warned against when he addressed the Ephesian elders. Anyone responsible for leading a small group in the church must be 'on guard'.

A vision for personal growth

Paul's secret in pastoral care was to have a vision of what God's people could become in Christ. He was aware of the potential not only of Christians in the church, but particularly of the leaders themselves: 'I commit you to God and to the word of his grace, which can build you up and give you an inheritance among all those who are sanctified' (Acts 20:32). I well remember when

I was a newly converted student at university, that I would suddenly become aware of certain leaders of the Christian group taking a special interest in me. I would be invited to their rooms for coffee, taken for long walks, given extra jobs to do in the college group – leading prayer times, giving talks – with an older Christian alongside to guide and help. Eventually it dawned on me that I was being groomed and nurtured for leadership. Others were investing time in me because they saw the potential in my life for serving God. This is the sort of pastoral care that small group leaders are called to exercise, building lives for future ministry.

Such leadership involves hard work, especially in caring for the weak and distressed who can take up hours of time and effort. Paul knew this too: 'In everything I did, I showed you that by this kind of hard work we must help the weak, remembering the words the Lord Jesus himself said: "It is more blessed to give than receive" ' (Acts 20:35). When leaders encourage group members to share a pastoral, caring ministry within their small groups, they are helping them discover the blessing of God in their lives. Conversely, the leader who holds every aspect of ministry to himself is, in a most selfish way, hindering the enrichment of his group members, who would receive more and more in their service of others. It is again the principle of the cross. Because Jesus was prepared to fall into the ground and die, like a seed, he opened the way for a mighty harvest (John 12:24). He said, 'Whoever serves me must follow me; and where I am, my servant also will be. My Father will honour the one who serves me' (John 12:26).

Specialist groups

Not all small groups are based on a programme of Bible study and prayer. Some gather on the basis of common gifts which are used to serve the church as a whole. These can become the primary points of fellowship for some group members, and the leaders need to be appointed with the same degree of care that would be shown in the appointment of other home group leaders. These specialist groups can be the source of healing, friendship and support for those who might otherwise be threatened in the sharing situation of a home group. Thus a group of singers and musicians may form their own specialist small group, in order to lead worship in church. Those with a gift of dance, or banner-making, may do the same thing. Usually, the members of such groups will belong to their own home groups and will only come together for prayer and practise as they minister to the wider church.

If a specialist worship group becomes detached from the main-stream of home group life, it can easily become an eccentric group, gathered primarily for performance, and on the basis of technical skills. This can often be a recipe for disaster. Such a group can easily highlight the tension between those church members who prefer traditional music in worship and those who hanker after newer songs and choruses. If the church has a strong musical tradition, with a choir and organist, there is every likelihood that rivalry and bad feeling will be expressed. I was invited to preach in one notable church in Birmingham. As I stood to begin my sermon, the robed choir stood too, then with due solemnity, filed out of church. 'Don't worry,' the curate said to me in an obvious stage whisper, 'they always do that. They're not objecting to you personally.' As the service proceeded I could not refrain from a sharp comment about walking out on the word of God. The final hymns and songs were led by a small singing group who took over in the absence of the choir. The sense of division and conflict was evident to everyone present; the sense of worship was destroyed rather than enhanced.

There are practical answers to such evident disorder. The leadership of any smaller group in the church, that comes together to lead in worship, must be submitted to the overall spiritual leadership of the congregation. It must not operate apart from the controlling influence (under God) of the pastor and his lay leaders (deacons, elders or church council). Ideally, an overall musical director should preside over the various smaller groups, which might include organist and choir, instrumentalists, singing group and dance group. The leader of each of these groups should be responsible for the prayer life, the programmes, the church and outside bookings, of his or her group. But above all, the leader must teach and encourage so that the group's ability and willingness to serve God and his people is never lost.

Having been an organist and choirmaster in a number of churches, as well as curate or vicar in others, I know how easily 'prima donna' attitudes take over. The worship groups are there only to serve. That is, after all, a primary meaning of the Greek word 'to worship'. If they are to serve God and the whole church, all the worship groups – whatever their specialist task – must submit to the overall spiritual leadership of the church.

3
Unwrapping the Spirit's gifts

The group's understanding

An understanding of how we experience God's Spirit is fundamental for sharing in and leading a small, home group. With regard to this understanding, the group may be in one of four possible situations:

- The members of the home group are all baptised, believing Christians, enjoying God's forgiveness, but longing for a release of his power in their lives through a fresh baptism with the Holy Spirit.
- The group may consist of some who have this further experience, and some who have not.
- Every member of the group may claim to have experienced the baptism of the Spirit, and all of them are exercising the gifts of the Spirit.
- The group may consist of Christians who believe that they were baptised with the Spirit when he first came to their lives, as they were born again, and together they are learning to claim more and more of his power and are gaining experience in the exercise of Holy Spirit gifts.

In the first sort of group there is a great danger of unhealthy introspection. All the members are discontent with their spiritual experience and fail to realise all that God has *already* given them by the Spirit. Instead of looking for a release of what is already within their lives, as they possess the Spirit, they are waiting for some great explosion of spiritual life which will reach them from outside their present experience.

In the second group there is the risk of division between those who 'have' this startling new experience of God, evidenced by certain spiritual gifts, and those who do not have such an experience. This speaks of first-class and second-class Christians, a concept unknown in the Bible. If we 'have received the Holy Spirit' of God then, by definition, we are his specially chosen, privileged children. Our standing with God is not defined by spiritual experiences, but by whether or not we are in a relationship to Jesus Christ through the Spirit.

In the third type of group, the 'baptism of the Spirit' can become a badge of membership. It is hard for someone to belong who has not had the same sort of experience in exactly the terms by which the other members of the group define it. The impression can be given that salvation is not solely on the grounds of Christ's death on the cross to win our forgiveness, but on that *plus* exactly the right sort of spiritual experience as defined by the Christian group to which you belong.

In the fourth group, there should be complete mutual acceptance. No wrong pressure need be put on any individual, since all are there because of the grace of Christ. There is no insistence on possessing particular spiritual gifts or experiences. All are children of God, meeting together in order to grow into his love and become more useful in his service. Some will have turned to the Lord gradually and will not even have had what they could call a 'conversion experience'. However, the love of the Spirit will be evidenced in the Christ-like beauty of their characters and personalities. Others may have had a notable experience of God at their conversion, which they describe in terms of a real baptism of love by the Holy Spirit. Yet others may have come to know Christ but then made little progress in the Christian life, perhaps because of lack of teaching or fellowship in their local church. As a result of this early failure, they may have taken a sudden or obvious step forward at some later stage, which they refer to as 'the baptism of the Spirit'. Within the open fellowship of the group, this way of describing their experience is no threat to others, since no one insists on it as a pattern for all to accept. Their early and somewhat unsatisfactory response to Christ is not dismissed as of no value at all but, rather, is seen as a sincere claiming of God's promise, anticipating the eventual full release of the Spirit's love and power.

The historical perspective

There has been confusion in the church about Holy Spirit gifts, because there have been two schools of thought regarding these gifts, even among Bible-believing Christians. Some have taught categorically that the miraculous gifts of the Spirit ceased with the apostles. 'In the apostolic age,' B B Warfield declared, 'the exception would be, not a church with, but a church without (miraculous) gifts. Everywhere, the Apostolic Church was marked out as itself a gift from God, by showing forth the possession of the Spirit in appropriate works of the Spirit – miracles of healing and miracles of power, miracles of knowledge, whether in the form of prophecy or of the discerning of spirits, miracles of speech, whether of the gift of tongues or of their interpretation. The Apostolic Church was characteristically a miracle-working church.' But, he continued, 'It was the characterising peculiarity of specifically the Apostolic Church, and it belonged therefore exclusively to the Apostolic age.' He added, 'The theologians of the post-Reformation era, a very clear-headed body of men, taught with great distinctness that the charismata ceased with the Apostolic age.' (*Counterfeit Miracles*, B B Warfield; The Banner of Truth Trust, 1972.)

Popular Bible teachers in the earlier part of this century took the same line. The noted Keswick speaker, W Graham Scroggie, wrote, 'Manifestations of the Spirit, therefore, were for a definite purpose, and for a limited period. The working of miracles, the visits of angels, the *general* speaking with Tongues, judicial acts such as the death of Ananias, Sapphira and Herod, the blessing of handkerchiefs, raising the dead, and other signs were for that transition period only, and when the purpose for which they were designed was accomplished, they ceased to operate as *evidential* signs.' (*The Baptism of the Spirit*, W Graham Scroggie; Pickering & Inglis Ltd.)

Paul does indeed say, 'where there are prophecies, they will cease; where there are tongues, they will be stilled; where there is knowledge, it will pass away' (1 Corinthians 13:8). But to quote this verse is to make only part of Paul's point. He goes on to say, 'but when perfection comes, the imperfect disappears' (13:10). Now, he argues, 'we know in part and we prophesy in part'(v 9), but this partial awareness pertains only until the perfection of Christ's rule is expressed. This will happen when he comes again, and all God's purposes are consummated in him.

All the while eminent Bible teachers were warning Christians not to expect Holy Spirit gifts in the contemporary church of the twentieth century, God was releasing those very gifts in the fast-growing Pentecostal churches. It all began at the turn of the century in the United States.

In 1906 there was a spiritual awakening in a stable that had been converted into a meeting house, in Azusa Street, Los Angeles. Under the ministry of the black pastor, William Seymour, this work of renewal continued for three years, and hundreds from all over the world came to be part of this special work of God. The meetings continued through the night, and many people received the blessing known to Pentecostals as 'Baptism in the Spirit', normally accompanied by the gift of speaking in tongues. Indeed, many believe that the modern Pentecostal movement was born in these gatherings, which were influenced by a number of people who had been significantly touched by God during the Welsh Revival of 1904 and 1905. Evan Roberts, a leader of this revival, had a great impact on an evangelical minister of the Church of England, Alexander Boddy, vicar of All Saints, Sunderland. Tongues speaking, scenes of ecstatic joy and all-night prayer times characterised his ministry and people from all over the country visited his church looking for a new experience of God's Spirit. However, so great was the opposition to this expression of pentecostal life from Anglican and Free Church leaders, that the movement never developed within mainstream churches. By the end of the First World War, the main

Pentecostal groups had been formed and a new denomination had begun.

As the mainstream churches rejected the witness of Pentecostal churches, the Holy Spirit gifts were limited for decades to that denomination. However, the dramatic growth of Pentecostal churches in pioneer missionary areas of the world as well as alongside mainstream churches in traditionally Christian lands, meant that their teaching had to be taken seriously, especially regarding the importance of spiritual gifts. For example, the growth of the Pentecostal churches in South America is such that, according to the church growth analyst, Peter Wagner, 'in 1900 there were approximately 50,000 evangelical Christians in Latin America; in 1930 over a million; in 1940 two million; in 1950 five million; in 1960 ten million and in 1970 twenty million.' (Peter Wagner, *Look Out, The Pentecostals Are Coming.*)

Eventually the insights of Pentecostal teaching came to Christians in the traditional churches through the so-called 'charismatic movement'. So-called because it is hardly a 'movement' planned by man. It can hardly be likened to an organisation like the Boy Scout Movement which was initiated by the driving force of its founder, Baden-Powell. The charismatic movement is rather a *moving* of the Spirit of God in many and varied ways in different parts of his church throughout the world. No one can pin down the moving of the Spirit of God, because he is sovereign in his dynamism and mobility. 'The wind blows wherever it pleases. You hear its sound, but you cannot tell where it comes from or where it is going' (John 3:8).

But although hard to define, many Christians in all the mainstream churches became aware both of the promise and the impact of the charismatic movement. The promise was conveyed in its title. The word 'charismatic' comes from the Greek word for grace. Thus the gifts of the Spirit associated with this movement are freely given for the benefit and blessing of God's people. They are all to do with God's generosity to his church. The impact of the movement has been most notably seen not in the gifts themselves, but in the way that the discovery of the gifts of the Spirit has affected the structure and ordering of so many churches. Although the home group Bible study or prayer meeting was known well before the new movement of the Spirit, the sense of every member of the church having a gift or gifts of the Spirit for the purpose of exercising mutual ministry within the body of Christ was previously not known. Now there is a 'must' about small groups in a local church, because there, supremely, every member of the group finds opportunity to use the Holy Spirit gifts and exercise the ministry, one to another.

When the gifts of the Spirit were first released among Christians in mainstream experience, there was no skill in handling them. They were perceived as playthings – new toys for God's children to enjoy. They were indulged in rather than used as means of ministry to others. Immature Christians became very excited about possessing them, and the gifts were used for display, as they were thought to be signs of God's special grace and favour on those to whom they were imparted. Consequently, many churches divided as 'charismatic Christians' made claims of superiority, and others felt threatened by their Christian brothers and sisters and neglected by God. The primary issue was frequently the gift of tongues, which Pentecostals had always taught was the required evidence that a Christian had been 'baptised in the Spirit'. Along with this, the understanding of the latter term was a divisive issue for years among Christian thinkers and theologians.

As Christians we need to hold in balance the teaching of the Bible and our experience of God's grace. It is tragic that, because his ways are so great and our minds so small, we have to argue even about his gifts and the promises that come from his grace! The controversy seems less sharp in the nineties than it was thirty years ago but, if small groups in church life are to be spheres of ministry where the Holy Spirit gifts can be exercised, it is helpful to understand the background to this debate.

Experiencing the Spirit

The Bible teaches quite clearly that when a person turns from sinful ways to trust in the living God, the Holy Spirit comes in re-creating power to live in that life, applying the forgiveness that Jesus Christ made possible through his death on the cross. That is what Jesus offered in his shorthand promise recorded as his first words in the earliest Gospel account: 'Repent, and believe the good news!' (Mark 1:15.) Peter offered the same at the end of his first public sermon on the day of Pentecost: 'Repent and be baptised, every one of you, in the name of Jesus Christ so that your sins may be forgiven. And you will receive the gift of the Holy Spirit. The promise is for you and your children and for all who are far off – for all whom the Lord our God will call.' (Acts 2:38–39.) Quite clearly, Peter expected an immediate pouring out of the Holy Spirit as soon as the conditions of repentance and faith were met. No one else would have to wait as the apostles and their friends had waited for the promise of Jesus to be fulfilled at the historic Pentecost event. That happening was unique and unrepeatable, the culmination of centuries of Old Testament promise in the Feast of Pentecost. Once those floodgates of Holy Spirit love had been opened, Peter expected the filling of every believer's heart and life to be normal Christian experience.

Jesus had anticipated this when he invited people to himself at the Feast of Tabernacles: ' "If a man is thirsty, let him come to me and drink. Whoever believes in me, as the Scripture has said, streams of living water will flow from within him." By this he meant the Spirit, whom those who believed in him were later to receive. Up to that time the Spirit had not been given, since Jesus had not yet been glorified.' (John 7:37–39.) Jesus was glorified in his death, and it was this that changed the way in which sinners can know their God. In Old Testament days he could be known in an external way through the word that was *outside* themselves. After Jesus died on the cross, and following Pentecost, God is known *within* our experience through the Holy Spirit being given to us. Jeremiah had prophesied it long ago: ' "I will put my law in their minds and write it on their hearts. I will be their God, and they will be my people. No longer will a man teach his neighbour, or a man his brother, saying, 'Know the Lord,' because they will all know me, from the least of them to the greatest," declares the Lord. "For I will forgive their wickedness and will remember their sins no more." ' (Jeremiah 31:33–34.)

Knowing God through Jesus, with sins forgiven and with his presence made real at the centre of our experience by the Holy Spirit, is the essential reality of what it means to become a Christian. Again and again in the New Testament this reality is described in terms of possessing the Holy Spirit. Indeed, Paul goes so far as to say, 'If anyone does not have the Spirit of Christ, he does not belong to Christ' (Romans 8:9). He uses many strong verbs to indicate the relationship of the believer with the Holy Spirit:

- 'the Spirit of life set me free' (Romans 8:2)
- 'the mind controlled by the Spirit is life and peace' (Romans 8:6)
- 'you . . . are controlled . . . by the Spirit, if the Spirit of God lives in you' (Romans 8:9)
- 'Christ is in you' (Romans 8:10)
- 'the Spirit of him who raised Jesus from the dead is living in you' (Romans 8:11).

When we add to these statements the imagery of our bodies individually, and the body of the church corporately, being the temple or dwelling place of God's Holy Spirit (1 Corinthians 3:16; 6:19), we see that in that dramatic moment when the human heart opens up to receive the presence of God's love, bringing about a veritable new birth at the spiritual level of human life, the Holy Spirit of God takes up permanent residence in our lives. Jesus himself *commanded* such new birth: 'I tell you the truth, unless a man is born again, he cannot see the kingdom of God' (John 3:3), and personally *guaranteed* the permanence of the presence of the Holy Spirit: 'I will ask the Father, and he will give you another Counsellor to be with you for ever – the Spirit of truth' (John 14:16–17).

'Further' experience?

Some schools of thought suggest that despite these strong promises, we do not have all the power nor all the gifts of the Holy Spirit when we first turn to Christ. Therefore, it is argued, the true believer must seek a further life-changing experience of the Holy Spirit, described as the 'baptism of the Holy Spirit'. This is clearly a scriptural term. John the Baptist said of Jesus, 'He will baptise you with the Holy Spirit and with fire' (Luke 3:16) and, shortly before his ascension into heaven, Jesus said to the disciples, 'John baptised with water, but in a few days you will be baptised with the Holy Spirit' (Acts 1:5). From this, some have deduced that there is a subsequent experience, *after* new birth, which gives Christians power for ministry and releases for their use the Holy Spirit gifts. Instances cited in the Acts of the Apostles, of people opening up to the working of the Spirit subsequent to their first awareness of his grace, are taken to confirm this view. For example, in Acts 8, people in Samaria had 'accepted the word of God' (v 14) but they had 'simply been baptised into the name of the Lord Jesus' (v 16). So when the apostles arrived from Jerusalem, 'Peter and John placed their hands on them, and they received the Holy Spirit' (v 17). Later, at Ephesus, Paul found some disciples who had received only John's baptism. He asked them, ' "Did you receive the Holy Spirit when you believed?" They answered, "No, we have not even heard there is a Holy Spirit" ' (Acts 19:2). Paul then baptised them into the name of the Lord Jesus and placed his hands on them. 'The Holy Spirit came on them, and they spoke in tongues and prophesied' (Acts 19:6).

These and other scriptures are taken as models for an expectation of the release and power of the Holy Spirit *after* an initial response to the word of God. But clearly these disciples had a totally inadequate understanding of the Spirit's person, presence and power. They had accepted God's promise as far as they understood it, but their basic position was that of ignorance of the true potential of God's power and love in their lives. This is surely the reason why so many believers are driven to seek a further experience, a new baptism, a second blessing – call it what you will. They are simply unaware of what it means to have all the power and love of our creator God living at the centre of their experience. They do not realise that if they possess the Giver of spiritual gifts, then potentially all the gifts are theirs too. They simply have to be claimed, as they are required in

God's service, and as they are released by God's sovereignty. It is because of ignorance of all that is available for Christian living, that many Christians are driven from the dryness and ineffectiveness of their spiritual lives, to seek something further from God.

Appropriating the Spirit's resources

Of course, even when we do know all that God longs to give us by his Spirit, our lives are so small and our faith so restrictive that we often fail to claim all that there is to receive. Consequently we spend our lives hungering and thirsting for righteousness (Matthew 5:6) but fail to remember the promise of Jesus attached to such longing for more and more of God: 'for they will be filled' (v 6). We grumble at our poor performance as disciples of Jesus; we groan for more of God; but we fail to believe him and his promise of fullness. The fact is that all the resources we can ever need *are given to us the moment we are born again by the Spirit of God*. This is God's supreme gift to our lives and all we have to do is unpack more and more of all that we have been given. Sometimes we make slow progress, untying a knot here and pulling aside some paper there, but gradually God's generous presents open up to us. At other times the revelation of God's provision is sudden and dramatic, and we take a huge step of new discovery in all that he has provided for us by his Spirit.

The idea of appropriating all of the Holy Spirit's power in just one giant step does not seem to tie in with scripture or experience. Clearly, there is one moment when we *receive* the Spirit, and that is surely what Jesus promised would happen to the disciples at Pentecost as they were 'baptised with the Holy Spirit' (Acts 1:5). But subsequent to that the disciples experienced many new encounters, many fresh fillings, as their moment by moment walk in the Spirit continued. After the prayer of the gathered church in Acts 4, 'they were all filled with the Holy Spirit and spoke the word of God boldly' (Acts 4:31). This was not a new Pentecost, but simply a fresh filling of power in answer to believing prayer. When Paul encountered Bar-Jesus, a Jewish sorcerer and false prophet in Paphos, he spoke vehemently against him as he was 'filled with the Holy Spirit' (Acts 13:9). This was not a new conversion for Paul, but simply a fresh empowering, a new discovery of Holy Spirit resources, as he continued his missionary work.

The New Testament picture, then, is of an initial outpouring of the Spirit when a person repents and believes in Jesus Christ; after that there are many new fillings as the relationship with God develops. When Paul says, 'be filled with the Spirit' (Ephesians 5:18), his meaning is, 'go on being filled' – constantly, frequently, regularly. It is as though the believer is to have many 'baptisms' with the Holy Spirit, and in his commentary on 1 Corinthians, Charles Hodge speaks in these terms: 'Any communication of the Holy Spirit is called a baptism because the Spirit is said to be poured out, and those upon whom he is poured out, whether in his regenerating, sanctifying, or inspiring influences, are said to be baptised.' (*The First Epistle to the Corinthians*, Charles Hodge. Banner of Truth Trust, 1958.)

Learning to use the gifts

Just as there is an immense variety of spiritual experience, so there is of gifts. The key thing to remember is that they are always given in and through people. Thus the meeting together in a small group is the ideal situation for learning to express the gifts of the Spirit. The gifts are for the benefit of the whole church; any word or message that is given to a smaller group must be communicated to the wider church family as well. Not everyone has confidence, however, to speak in a large meeting of the gathered church; most people find it easier to speak or share in the smaller group.

In his advice to the New Testament churches Paul does not insist that every single person is present for every meeting, but he does emphasise that every meeting is for the good of the whole church: 'When you come together, everyone has a hymn, or a word of instruction, a revelation, a tongue or an interpretation. All of these must be done for the strengthening of the church' (1 Corinthians 14:26). Only when a church fellowship is small numerically, would it be possible for everyone to be present at one time. Even so, in our days of mobility with people travelling further and more frequently than before on day-to-day business, it is virtually impossible for the whole church to 'come together' with every member present. However, in its smaller manifestation, the local home group, it is far more likely that a large proportion of the usual group will be committed to attend regular meetings.

The sense of unity and togetherness provided by a group that meets regularly and whose members are committed to each other, is as essential for the expression of spiritual gifts as the fact that the individuals possess gifts. In my own case, it was some years after claiming the gifts of the Spirit that I was able to belong to a group of Christians who were of one mind in longing for the gifts to be used. I didn't grow in understanding or in confident use of the gifts of the Spirit until I joined that group and the right circumstances prevailed. The faith and expectation of a local church fellowship hinders or helps its individual members to grow in this respect. The key factor here is leadership. For gifts to flourish and to be used well, the leader of the local church must be actively seeking God's best will for that church in the release of spiritual gifts – not becoming wrongly preoccupied with them but certainly not neglecting them.

I remember going to the church council of St John's, Harborne, as spiritual gifts were beginning to be expressed during the monthly Sunday evening Communion service. A few in the congregation were troubled at what was beginning to happen, though I knew of hundreds in the fellowship who spoke in tongues and were beginning to manifest other gifts. I had to ask the council to back my leadership as gifts came to be openly used. 'After all,' I said, 'if we make as little progress in this matter as we have done in the last four and a half years since I became Vicar, there will be little outward evidence of charismatic renewal in the church at all.' Up to that time, individual Christians exercised Holy Spirit gifts privately in their lives, and in informal groups with praying friends, but few felt free to express themselves in the main prayer times of the church or in Sunday services. This was because the issue was controversial, and those who were becoming familiar with the exercise of gifts in other churches, or at charismatic rallies, did not wish to cause a division in our church. They did not wish to appear to be the 'haves', so that they would seem to be superior to those who did not yet have the gifts in a conscious way. It was entirely a motive of love and a desire for unity in the fellowship, that hindered the confident release of gifts in the church. We were moving slowly in the Spirit, but I could see that we were at a point of breakthrough and I needed backing from the council for my leadership, since I was as inexperienced as anybody else in handling such a situation. As I pointed out to the members of the council, I needed support for my *mistakes*, as much as for any wisdom and help in controlling the situation, under God. 'If I make a mistake,' I said, 'you can be the first to exercise the Christian privilege of being able to forgive me, in Christ's name. Then I can tell any critics that no doubt they are correct in saying I handled things badly, but it is not a serious problem, because I already have the promise of the PCC's forgiveness – in advance!'

This question of being able to cope with mistakes is an important one, as groups, large or small, begin to exercise spiritual gifts. Just as it is a very demanding thing for some Christians to pray aloud in public for the first time, so it is costly to step out for God in using a gift. There is always the fear that one will misinterpret what God wants, dry up or seem foolish. Frequently a person will come to the leader, after a meeting, with an interpretation or a message that they were too hesitant to share. The leader should then make a note of what the contribution was about, and the context in which it should have been spoken, and encourage the person to speak out the next time there is an opportunity to do so in a public meeting. Such a person is never to be castigated but is always to be encouraged to have another try and to grow in confidence. If the 'feel' of the whole fellowship is warm and expectant, and the leadership is genuinely encouraging, gifts will soon begin to flow.

Because the gifts of the Spirit are released from God's grace, and are not commanded by people or controlled by human skills, it is important for the leader of the meeting to encourage everyone present to *expect* God to move by his Spirit and to release the Spirit's gifts through those present. Equally, an encouragement to speak out and contribute to the meeting is not a licence for self-display. When a group begins to move in the Spirit, it is often the spiritually immature who try to dominate the meeting. They claim spiritual gifts and push themselves forward in seeking to express them. Such claims have to be tested, and usually the onus lies with the leader of the group to make sure that the meeting does not get out of hand. How this works out in practice is described in chapter 4.

Gifts to equip the church

The Holy Spirit gives an immense variety of gifts in the church. Some of these are described in passing in other chapters, but it is important to see the whole range of spiritual gifts which God is longing to impart in and through his people, and which we are mostly so slow to appropriate. It was Lord Coggan who urged Christians to 'possess their possessions', since the only way God's gifts for the church may be experienced is through individual members of the body of Christ laying hold of them, and then using them in the service of God and of other people.

The New Testament lists an immense variety of Holy Spirit gifts and in Ephesians 4 Paul lists different groups of people who have special ministries that represent God's gifts to the church: 'It was he who gave some to be apostles, some to be prophets, some to be evangelists, and some to be pastors and teachers, to prepare God's people for works of service, so that the body of Christ may be built up until we all reach unity in the faith and in the knowledge of the Son of God and become mature, attaining to the whole measure of the fulness of Christ' (Ephesians 4:11–13). We will look at each of these ministries in turn.

Apostles
In the church today ministry has become so stylised, and so much part of the bureaucratic system of many of the mainstream churches, that there is very little comparison with the early church in our patterns of ministry. Clearly, the first apostles were unique in that they were eye-witnesses of Jesus and had particular significance in founding the first churches. Writing to Christians

at Ephesus, Paul says: 'You are no longer foreigners and aliens, but fellow-citizens with God's people and members of God's household, built on the foundation of the apostles and prophets, with Christ Jesus himself as the chief cornerstone' (Ephesians 2:19–20).

But we still have pioneers and church planters today. *Apostle* means 'sent one'; we take its Latin equivalent, *missio*, and call such pioneers 'missionaries'. They may be men or women whom a home church sends out to other countries – traditionally, we have used the word to describe an overseas initiative. Increasingly, however, churches are being planted in Great Britain too. A group of Christians moved from St John's, Harborne, across a busy main road that marked the parish boundary, to establish a new work in a neighbouring parish. A number bought homes and transferred all their commitment to a different part of the city. They sent their children to local schools, identifying with the ninety or so per cent of pupils who were black. They befriended their neighbours and, by a variety of means, sought to build friendships in their new community. Success has been measurable even if slow and small-scale. But the quality of the work and the spirit in which it has been undertaken, is apostolic.

Other families and individuals have worked in a more typically missionary way with long-established missionary societies. One family went to a Latin American shanty area and also lived among wealthy middle-class people in the cities of South America. Starting with no congregation at all they have planted churches which, by God's grace, are flourishing today. Another journeyed hundreds of miles across rough land and swollen rivers to reach a remote pygmy tribe with the gospel of Christ. Apostolic outreach is happening all over the world, and those with gifts of church-planting are God's gifts to the church.

Such ministry, as we have seen, is not limited to the signed-up staff of a missionary society. The dramatic growth of the church in Seoul, South Korea, pastored by Dr Paul Yonggi Cho, shows how every member of that church is expected to plant new groups as they move out into new neighbourhoods. In *Successful Home Cell Groups* (Logos International, 1981) he says, 'Each one of my members becomes a missionary to his own neighbourhood and an agent for revival in that neighbourhood.' He tells how he relied on the leadership of women in his fast growing church and describes how they plant churches by drawing other women from the supermarkets, as they make contact and listen to their problems there. Others spend time riding up and down in the lifts of the tower blocks in which they live, making friends by offering to carry people's shopping, and eventually inviting them to the newly-formed church fellowship nearby. These are not professional missionaries planting new churches, but ordinary church members with apostolic zeal and an overwhelming desire to obey Christ's final commission to his church.

Prophets

Prophets in the New Testament have no exact equivalent today. Theirs was a travelling ministry of teaching and encouragement, bringing a message directly from God into the life of the newly established local churches. It seems to have been the sort of ministry that is often exercised at a church residential weekend, where a gifted visiting preacher has opportunity to bring an outside dimension into the ongoing life of the local church. It is quite a distinct ministry from that of the visiting evangelist, and clearly has a more direct, challenging impact than is possible for the settled pastor or teacher to have.

Sometimes this ministry has been confused with that of the prophets in the Old Testament. Their writings form a settled part of the canon of Scripture and it is quite evident that in comparison the proclamation of the New Testament prophet was peripheral and transitory. No great prophetic tomes survive and their ministry did not have the national dimension of God speaking directly through them to the whole people of Israel. They ministered in the smaller groupings of newly established local churches, 'forth-telling' the word rather than 'fore-telling' the future. The latter aspect is, however, present in the New Testament at a personal level. The prophet Agabus warned Paul of danger ahead, as he journeyed to Jerusalem (Acts 21:10–14). He took Paul's belt and gave a visual, enacted word to him, not dissimilar to the vivid prophetic actions of Old Testament prophets. The pictorial element of his prophecy also characterises the informal prophetic words and pictures that have become a mark of ministry in many renewed Christian groups. Agabus used Paul's belt to tie his own hands and his feet and said: 'The Holy Spirit says, "In this way the Jews of Jerusalem will bind the owner of this belt and will hand him over to the Gentiles" ' (Acts 21:11). Agabus gave no word of command with the prophecy and, despite the entreaty of his other friends, Paul still continued his journey to Jerusalem. He was now even more clearly aware of danger and chose to face it, knowing God's power to keep him safe.

Evangelists

There is, similarly, little room for the ministry of full-time evangelists in British mainstream churches. Those who are set aside for this task tend to be supported by specially established evangelistic trusts. They are used by churches with an evangelistic vision, but few who use them count the cost of their ministry and give them adequate monetary reward. A full-time, gifted evangelist on our staff at St John's has been widely used by other churches, student groups and schools, but has not succeeded in raising even one fifth of a modest living wage for himself and his wife, from all his ministry outside our church. In the Anglican church, some dioceses employ a missioner, but the ministry of evangelism has remained the Cinderella of the church and has been limited largely to that of the Church Army.

Clearly, not all evangelism has to be performed by full-time paid agents. Members of local churches who are not in full-time ministry can express their evangelistic gifts within the framework and programme of the local church. Paul Yonggi Cho describes his basic evangelistic policy as 'cell group evangelism'. This obviously suits the patterns of South Korean society. He criticises the concept of door to door evangelism, calling it 'a confrontation type of evangelism. It invites resistance, as Christians resist Jehovah's Witnesses and Mormons.' Yonggi Cho emphasises cell group evangelism because it is the place where *real* life is to be found in the neighbourhood. By contrast, we find the opposite is true in our evangelism in Birmingham. Home group evangelism is felt to be sharply confrontational. Outsiders invited to such meetings find them threatening and church members are ill at ease in sharing their faith in a context that seems designed for social pleasantries. Consequently our main thrust is through door to door evangelism which works far more successfully. The evangelistic team forms a small group of those either with the gift of evangelism or willing to 'do the work of an evangelist' (2 Timothy 4:5) and over the years the door to door witness has proved to be our most effective way of using God's gifts in the extension of the Gospel.

The work of regular church organisations, particularly for young people, must not be forgotten in an enthusiasm for developing small groups in which mutual ministry can be expressed among adults. Frequently the teams of leaders of both uniformed and non-uniformed youth and children's organisations provide support for each other in their youth evangelism, which in many cases is an alternative to the fellowship otherwise provided by a home group.

Another vital area of evangelism is among the elderly. Sometimes this is achieved through Darby and Joan clubs which bring men and women together on a social basis, with occasional evangelistic talks injected into the programme. We find it best to follow the home group pattern, particularly with the older women in our parish. A team of speakers with evangelistic gifts use those gifts to speak to the groups and bring many to faith; others with gifts of teaching can then follow up their work. The older men prefer to follow a more ordered teaching programme, but within it the work of evangelism is done by men bringing their friends to hear the gospel, and by gifted evangelists speaking at their meetings. All of these smaller groups, whether for young or old in the community, have friendship, mutual care and support at the heart of their programmes. They enable a gospel outreach to take place and gifts of evangelism to be expressed, which could not be achieved either through the regular Sunday church services or through any sort of large-scale rally evangelism.

Pastors

The pastoral task dominates the concept of ministry in the local church, because it is performed by the ordained person set aside by the church for full-time supervision of the needs of God's people in the local church. I was taught at theological college that any one person can minister fully, in this pastoral way, only to some two hundred people in the course of a lifetime. It is the concept of 'one-man-band ministry', with one minister attempting to fulfil all the pastoral and leadership tasks, that is so strongly challenged by the biblical insights of the charismatic renewal.

Undoubtedly, it is the image of the pastor that gives the clearest idea of what ministry in the New Testament is all about. Jesus described himself as 'the Good Shepherd' (John 10:11) and, in speaking of his mission 'to seek and to save the lost', he used the picture of a shepherd willing to 'leave the ninety-nine in the open country', to 'go after the lost sheep until he finds it' (Luke 15:4). Finding the one lost sheep is the occasion for great rejoicing both for himself and his friends and neighbours. Jesus presents this as a picture of the 'rejoicing in heaven over one sinner who repents' (Luke 15:7).

Simon Peter is commissioned to the pastoral task as he is reinstated by Jesus after his denial, and with each profession of love that Peter makes, Jesus commits him to a different aspect of the shepherd's task: 'feed my lambs' (John 21:15), 'take care of my sheep' (21:16), 'feed my sheep' (21:17). It is not surprising that in his first letter Peter frequently uses pastoral images, describing Jesus as 'the Chief Shepherd' (1 Peter 5:4). But in this passage it is the elders in the church who are the under-shepherds and, as we have already seen, eldership in the New Testament was a shared task. In appointing elders in the church, the apostles established a structure very different from the modern idea of a local church being a congregation served by one or two paid pastors.

Again, it is the small group network within the local congregation that enables all those with pastoral gifts to express their ministry. There are, however, many people in a congregation who, while clearly possessing pastoral gifts, could never undertake the many varied tasks of oversight required of the full-time pastor. Even when the pastoral task is shared by others, the leadership of the full-time presbyter is unquestionably required for the care of God's flock. 'Be shepherds of God's flock that is under your care, serving as overseers – not because you must, but because you are willing, as God wants you to be, not greedy for money, but eager to serve; not lording it over those entrusted to you, but being examples to the flock.' (1 Peter 5:2–3.)

To have this ministry is to possess a gift from God. To allow it to be exercised requires a careful structuring of the congregation, in small groups, so that many leaders can share the pastoral task. Not that the small group leader is the only one to share in this aspect of eldership. He or she will encourage every group member to share in the pastoral task, visiting the sick, listening to the afflicted, supporting those who are lame and struggling in their walk with God. Care needs to be taken here, of course. For example, the leader's responsibility may be to prevent everyone visiting a patient in hospital on the same day! A rota can ensure that everyone has a turn, and that the patient's recovery is not hindered by over zealous visiting.

Teachers

Many congregations have professional schoolteachers and other skilled educationists in their membership, but their structures do not allow the gifts and skills of technically competent teachers to be expressed. Traditionally they have played a vital role in Sunday Schools, but few churches use such talents in adult education. It is not everyone's call to share the pulpit ministry, since this is a specialised task and needs a degree of continuity if it is to be purposefully accomplished. A relationship is built up between those called to a regular pulpit teaching ministry and the congregation itself, which is lost if so many share the task that the primary teaching elder does not have opportunity to teach regularly himself.

This is another problem solved in the smaller group – not just the home group, but in groups of enquirers or young Christians who need basic teaching either at the pre-evangelistic level or in the basics of faith. Wedding and baptism preparation courses and, in some churches, confirmation classes, can be taught by members of the congregation with a teaching gift who are not necessarily elders or full-time staff. Paul reminded the Ephesian elders in his address at Miletus, that he had taught 'publicly and from house to house' (Acts 20:20). He combined teaching on the larger public occasion with ministry in the smaller group as well – a perfect example for us to follow.

Congregational ministry

In his narrative of God's 'people-gifts' for the church, Paul adds his vision of the outcome of the exercise of the ministry of apostles, prophets, evangelists, pastors and teachers. It is that *the whole body* of Christ should become engaged in ministry. God gave the gifts of these ministries 'to prepare God's people for works of service, so that the body of Christ may be built up' (Ephesians 4:12).

Here, beyond any doubt, is the description of the immense variety of ministries within the body of Christ. The picture of a Christian, isolated and alone, detached from others in the church, is utterly foreign to the New Testament. The idea of the church as a building in which pilgrims gather for a 'me and my God experience', is denied by all the New Testament's images for the church, which is presented by St Paul as a living, growing building, a body and a bride. His metaphors are somewhat mixed at times, but all speak of relationship and interdependence of the different elements: 'In him the whole building is joined together and rises to become a holy temple in the Lord. And in him you too are being built together to become a dwelling in which God lives by his Spirit' (Ephesians 2:21–22). In Ephesians 4:4 he says, 'There is one body'. Later he commands husbands to love their wives 'as Christ loved the church and gave himself up for her to make her holy' (Ephesians 5:25) and it is this body, the church, that is to be built up as the gifts of ministry are exercised within it.

The variety of Holy Spirit gifts is developed in the other lists that Paul gives in 1 Corinthians 12 and Romans 12. The latter is extremely practical, and includes the gifts of encouragement, giving money, leadership, showing mercy and practising hospitality. As well as describing the gifts, Paul also tells us how they should be used: 'Do not think of yourself more highly than you ought, but rather think of yourself with sober judgment, in accordance with the measure of faith God has given you' (Romans 12:3). The right attitude of heart is essential for proper use of each gift. If your gift is to contribute money, then it must be done 'generously'. If it is leadership, then you must 'govern diligently'. If it is showing mercy, then 'do it cheerfully' (12:8).

Not all of these are the kind of spiritual gifts that have been emphasised in the charismatic renewal, but they are to be expected when Christians obey Paul's call in the opening verses of this chapter: 'I urge you, brothers, in view of God's mercy, to offer your bodies as living sacrifices, holy and pleasing to God – which is your spiritual worship' (12:1). Furthermore, these practical gifts enable the interdependence of the body of Christ to be demonstrated and realised: 'Just as each of us has one body with many members, and these members do not all have the same function, so in Christ we who are many form one body, and each member belongs to all the others' (12:4–5).

4
Every-member ministry

The New Testament's picture of the church is one of dynamic life. It is the potential of every small group in the church to become part of this as a living, active, interdependent, varied and unified organism, seething with the very life of God himself, by the Spirit. It is a group that acknowledges Jesus as Lord, in which the members care for each other. There 'should be no division in the body, but . . . its parts should have equal concern for each other. If one part suffers, every part suffers with it' (1 Corinthians 12:25–26). In this passage Paul intertwines the twin themes of unity and variety. Far from the expression of Holy Spirit gifts being the source of division in the church, they are in fact the means of expressing true, organic unity. The members or 'parts' of the body are there, united by the Spirit, with the purpose of releasing the gifts for each other's benefit. 'Now you are the body of Christ, and each one of you is a part of it' (1 Corinthians 12:27).

Other groups of humans find their common life in an outside, unifying purpose – perhaps some sport or shared interest in music, French literature or Winnie the Pooh. The group of Christians finds the Holy Spirit to be its unifying factor, and the release of the Spirit's gifts its means of expressing this shared life. Just as each part of the human body has its unique function within the whole, so each member of the body of Christ has its special part to play and its special gift to release for the good of others.

As the gifts listed in Romans 12 are for use by people who are surrendered to God as 'living sacrifices', so the Holy Spirit gifts promised in 1 Corinthians 12 are for those surrendered to Jesus as Lord – 'and no-one can say "Jesus is Lord," except by the Holy Spirit' (1 Corinthians 12:3). Paul contrasts the barrenness of pagan religion with a living relationship with God through faith in Jesus Christ. He reminds the Christians of Corinth of their former state: 'You know that when you were pagans, somehow or other you were influenced and led astray to dumb idols' (1 Corinthians 12:2). In other words, you were carried along like rubbish in the gutter, unable to control your destiny, and with no voice to guide you. How different now that you are in a relationship with God, through faith in Jesus Christ! Now you have the Holy Spirit in your life, you can talk sense with God, and affirm that 'Jesus is Lord'. More than that, he is a living God, not a dumb idol, and he will speak *to* you and *through* you.

A way of developing our ability to listen to the voice of God, as he directs Christian ministry in specific and personal ways, is described by Peter Lawrence, an Anglican vicar in Birmingham, in his book *The Hot Line* (Eastbourne: Kingsway, 1990). He suggests, as the publisher's blurb tells us, that 'Learning to recognise, receive, test and give "words" from God is just like learning any other discipline. There are no easy answers and there is no cheap grace.' His book will certainly help any Christian to listen more closely to God as he speaks by his Spirit today.

In 1 Corinthians 12 the gifts concern 'speaking by the Spirit of God' (v 3), *to him* in praise, and *to the church* with messages that are given under his direct inspiration. But before listing the varied gifts, Paul develops his theme of unity and variety. He speaks of 'different kinds of gifts' (v 4), 'different kinds of service' (v 5) and 'different kinds of working' (v 6), but confirms that 'God works all of them in all men' (v 6). Absolutely everyone is involved, and the gifts for ministry are as varied as the people through whom they are manifested. The full list which follows emphasises the variety: the message of wisdom, the message of knowledge, faith, gifts of healing, miraculous powers, prophecy, distinguishing between spirits, speaking in different kinds of tongues, the interpretation of tongues (vs 8–10). And no one is left out in the distribution of these Holy Spirit gifts: 'to each one the manifestation of the Spirit is given' (v 7). They are given 'to one and to another'. He gives them to each one, just as he determines' (v 11). 'The body is a unit, though it is made up of many parts' (v 12).

The variety of gifts and the diversity of people who express them opens the possibility of tremendous disorder in the use of the gifts in church life. Indeed, many Christians see them *only* in terms of potential disunity, because they fail to understand how the Lord of the church expresses his sovereignty as the gifts are released. Paul speaks of God himself as the unifying factor. The gifts may be infinitely varied, but they come from 'the same Spirit' (v 4), 'the same Lord' (v 5) and 'the same God' (v 6). The unity is that of God the Holy Trinity – dynamic, powerful, mobile to be sure, but secure and certain as well. The gifts are 'the manifestation of the Spirit' (v 7). They come 'through the Spirit' (v 8). They are all 'of the same Spirit' (v 8). So 'All these are the work of one and the same Spirit, and he gives them to each one, just as he determines' (v 11).

How then are we to understand the individual gifts and encourage their use in the small group and the church? The list can be divided up in a number of ways, but in terms of practical outworking in the life of a group of believers, it is helpful to see them as providing the power to *say*, the power to *know*, and the power to *do* things for God.

The power to say

Prophecy

Prophecy is a primary speech gift (1 Corinthians 12:10). In 1 Corinthians 14:1 Paul singles this gift out among all the others: 'Follow the way of love and eagerly desire spiritual gifts, especially the gift of prophecy.' The person with this gift is commended because 'he who prophesies edifies the church' (v 4) and, however much the apostle wished that everyone should speak in tongues, Paul said, 'I would rather have you prophesy. He who prophesies is greater than one who speaks in tongues, unless he interprets, so that the church may be edified' (v 5).

Paul defines this gift as speaking to people 'for their strengthening, encouraging and comfort' (v 3). Prophecy is thus a giving of words from God to others in the local fellowship in a way that has a measurable effect on their lives. Each Christian is as strong as the group enables him to be, as strengthening words are spoken. Alone we can be weak and vulnerable, subject to the pressure of Satanic attack – as Jesus was, alone in the wilderness. Together, we are able to be mutually supportive, strong with a strength that is unavailable to us apart from the group of Christians to which we belong. Furthermore, in a threatening, accusing world, we find words of encouragement for our upbuilding when the gift of prophecy is expressed. Since Satan is described as 'the accuser of brethren', it is the word of prophecy that counters his lies with God's word of encouragement. Also, as the Holy Spirit comes alongside us as an advocate, pleading God's cause in our lives (John 14:16) and representing the presence of Jesus with us and in us, so the word of prophecy performs the same function. The word of the 'comforter' brings us 'comfort' (1 Corinthians 14:3). In the early church, as we have seen, prophets with this ministry travelled around the churches, bringing God's strengthening word to them through their ministry.

The temptation when this gift is exercised in a small group is for self-display. Sometimes the person with a prophetic gift is sensitive and vulnerable. Without being merely attention-seeking, he or she can feel genuinely grateful for the sense of self-worth that is gained from being the vehicle through whom the prophetic word is given. Those who are naturally shy may not have the confidence to speak out in a larger church meeting, when the clergy and other elders are present. The small group provides this opportunity, but it also provides a chance for an individual to rule and manipulate the proceedings by delivering 'messages' that may not be from God at all.

Paul calls for discipline to be exercised by the leadership of the group when prophecies are being given. 'Two or three prophets should speak, and the others should weigh carefully what is said' (1 Corinthians 14:29). The meeting is clearly not to be taken over by an endless succession of prophetic contributions. The opportunity for others to 'weigh carefully what is said' needs to be given by those in charge of the meeting. There can be a form of piety that feels it is wrong to interrupt the flow that professes to be God's word to the meeting, whereas Paul suggests that *every* prophetic word should be considered, and presumably accepted or rejected then and there by those present. Obviously such weighing of a word can be done after the meeting is over, but it is often helpful to those with a prophetic gift to be present and to hear the reactions of others.

In my early days of belonging to such a small group, when the gifts of the Spirit were beginning to be exercised, it became very clear that not all 'prophetic' contributions were trustworthy. Some, couched in scriptural phraseology, were accusing in tone. This conflicted with Paul's teaching that 'everyone who prophesies speaks to men for their strengthening, encouragement and comfort' (1 Corinthians 14:3). I found that, from time to time, a picture would form in my mind, but the image was black and dark and I was not at ease sharing it with the praying group. As soon as I realised the possibility that this was either from myself or Satan, and resisted his influence, the dark picture would disappear. It soon became clear that any one of us when we speak can offer words that come from self, from Satan or from God. Before we speak we need to exercise discernment ourselves, so that the group can weigh our words. Once, a girl rushed to the front of a prayer time which was being held in church and made specific evil allegations against one of our respected members – who was sitting in the front row of the meeting. My colleague who was leading the meeting asked for her words to be tested by the whole gathering. No support was found for her accusing words, which had been presented in prophetic form, so he commanded the girl to return to her place and be silent. She withdrew to the very back of the church and, after a short while, left the meeting. When she was subsequently offered help, it emerged that she had a background of mental disorder, of which we had been previously unaware, and she was at the beginning of a breakdown.

Firm leadership is required in the smaller group no less than the large, so that false contributions are discerned and, within a close-knit fellowship, discipline and control can be expressed. It is, of course, just as important to encourage definite words from God, as it is to discourage items of self-display or Satanic delusion.

When a group becomes confident in handling the gift of prophecy, it is easy to forget that newcomers may never have experienced the use of spiritual gifts. What may seem customary and ordinary to regular members may seem unusual and strange to newcomers. It is essential that new members are put at ease and that procedures are explained from time to time, so that they do not seem to be esoteric happenings which only the initiated can understand. Indeed, some new members may need to be helped to claim gifts for themselves, so that they in turn become confident to minister and to share with others what God has given to them.

Perhaps it is even more important to be able to understand and interpret the prophetic word than it is to initiate the release of gifts in the first place. A hiatus may be reached once the gift has been released. No one knows quite what to do next! The leader, or the person who has given the prophetic word or picture, does not wish to dominate the meeting, so he or she keeps quiet, hoping that another person will take on the theme or explain what it seems that God may be saying to the group by his Spirit. Others are fearful of contributing wrongly, so they keep quiet. So instead of experiencing a purposeful moment of divine breakthrough, the whole group hovers in embarrassed silence, becoming more and more self-conscious rather than God conscious.

It is at such a point that the leader, or another mature Christian, could intervene, explaining exactly what is happening. There are several points of instruction that can be given to help the group forward, until it is at ease and experienced at coping with the prophetic gift:

- Point out the need to weigh the prophetic word.
- The leader may ask if any member of the group has already had a matching verse of scripture in his mind, perhaps

throughout the evening, and encourage him to speak it out.

- If the word given is in the form of a picture, the leader can do the same, asking if anyone might be in a position to develop the image, by sharing an understanding or insight that God has already given them.
- The group may need to understand that if the picture demands interpretation, more than one person may share different aspects of what the picture is saying to them.
- It may be helpful to point out that even contradictory interpretations should be given. The whole group can then weigh up the alternative possibilities of what the picture means, or the group may come to find that the apparently contradictory explanations are, in the end, complementary.
- The leader may suggest a time of silence, of quietly waiting on God. If the silence is introduced purposefully, it will be creative and not merely embarrassing.
- The group can be told the importance of sharing the word with the wider church, either at a larger meeting or by informing other small group leaders. Some in the group may have a pertinent prophetic word which has recently been given in another church meeting, or which confirms the one that has just been given.

From time to time a prophecy that has been given outside the fellowship of the local church, will suddenly be seen to be relevant in the local situation. We have had two notable examples of this happening in our church – one some years ago, and the other quite recently. At a time in the early seventies we were particularly indebted at St John's, Harborne, to the ministry of Jean Darnall, the American preacher and teacher. God has used her greatly in the British renewal scene, with her husband Elmer. She shared with us the prophetic picture of pockets of light shining and spreading all over Europe. Although this was given widely across the country in many churches and praying fellowships, a number of us felt it was of particular relevance to St John's.

The effect of such a prophecy is to guide the ventures that a church undertakes, and to provide priorities for choosing between different calls and ministries. Over the years that followed, doors opened for preaching and ministry tours with our choir and worship dance group, in Sweden, Denmark and Finland. In return we have also been able to receive into our church both small and large groups from those countries, and from Norway as well. There are churches operating in the 'Open to God' pattern in all those countries, and this bond of friendship has led to a joining up of churches and a spreading of Christ's light all over Scandinavia.

More recently the fulfilment of this vision has been seen in a remarkable way, spreading from St John's to a rural area of Northern Finland through links with a Swedish speaking Finnish Lutheran pastor, Johann Candelin. Having seen our choir and worship dance group on Finnish TV following one of our tours, he found himself suddenly aware of the potential for shared ministry within the body of Christ. He made arrangements to visit Birmingham and some other Anglican parish churches which had come into renewal. After his return, some two hundred young people were converted in his parish. Eventually, teams from this group were sent out to preach the gospel and bring encouragement to the churches in various Eastern European countries. St John's could never have reached these places itself, but that prophetic word has come true as different parts of Europe have been lit up with the gospel. And the St John's link has continued. Several of our former members, now ordained and serving in other churches, have taught each year at the summer youth camps of these Finnish Lutherans and, in 1990, Johann, his bishop Erik, and a party of leading Finnish Christians, visited Birmingham.

From this, we have seen that the outworking of a word of prophecy may take years to happen. Sometimes it is only recognised as the prophecy's outworking, at a fairly late stage of the programme. Currently, we are encouraged in Birmingham by a word of prophecy regarding young teenagers. We have a promise that many adults will be won to Christ through the testimony of many young teenagers who are to be converted in the coming years. To be inspired by such a prophecy stimulates our faith, prayer and effort in the task of teenage evangelism. It governs the decisions of the Church Council in funding youth projects. It guides us in the sort of gifts we look for in new staff members, and gives us confidence and hope as we go forward in the Lord's work. It does not mean that we repeatedly read out the word of prophecy, or constantly recall its message at our meetings. It does mean that we are not surprised when youth projects appear on our agendas; and we are aware of an overall pattern, inspired by God's Spirit, as the work develops.

For example, at St Germain's we have set up an 'Operation Gideon' venture jointly with British Youth for Christ, sponsoring young people who will work and witness in our parish over a four-year period. At no stage has anyone in the leadership used any word of prophecy to blackmail others into deciding to back the programme, presenting it as God's will for our church with success guaranteed by his prophetic word. The matter has never been discussed in these terms. However, as Vicar, I have been well aware of the prophecy as it has governed decision-making while the scheme was unfolded to us.

As I write this, the timing of this project has been delayed. But the Youth for Christ workers have been able to rent a suitable house in the parish and, though key youth workers from St Germain's have moved away, we are not disheartened. The word of instruction and the vision from God is sure. We must simply allow him to plan the timing for us as circumstances over-rule our original hopes and expectations. Over the next few years I expect to see God work as he has graciously promised.

Tongues and interpretation

In the early days of charismatic renewal, there was so much emphasis on this gift of the Spirit, that it became known as the 'tongues movement'! It was, after all, *the* gift insisted on by Pentecostal Christians as evidence of the baptism of the Holy Spirit. Many who wanted acceptance within renewal circles longed for this Holy Spirit gift above all. And yet, as we have seen, Paul clearly sees it as of secondary importance to the gift of prophecy. He is enthusiastic about the gift of tongues, as any grateful recipient of God's good gifts must be. He says, 'I would like every one of you to speak in tongues' (1 Corinthians 14:5), but the tongues gift is of limited value compared with prophecy. 'Anyone who speaks in a tongue does not speak to men but to God. Indeed, no-one understands him; he utters mysteries with his spirit' (14:2).

It is of smaller value than prophecy, only because it reaches fewer people in the church. In personal prayer devotion, it is of vital importance. It is a gift that not only indicates God's sovereignty as the giver but goes straight back to him in adoration, praise and purposeful intercession. It is both from God, and for God. It brings him glory. But in the church it has importance more for the individual than the group: 'He who speaks in a tongue edifies himself, but he who prophesies edifies the church' (1 Corinthians 14:4). So Paul concludes, 'I thank God that I speak in tongues more than all of you. But in the church I would rather speak five intelligible words to instruct others than ten thousand words in a tongue.' (14:18–19.) So, it is important to have the tongues issue in perspective. It is a good gift from God and is therefore not to be rejected. It is for the individual's upbuilding, and is therefore not to be despised. But the New Testament emphasis seems to be on its importance in the individual's prayer relationship with God.

In another place I have written about tongues as 'Baby Language': 'Some call tongues gibberish or gobbledegook! Yet when a baby gurgles in its pram and speaks apparently meaningless gibberish to its mother, and mother leans over the pram and returns the baby talk, there is a real communication of love. No one doubts that! No parent or baby would wish to be without it.' (*Renew us by your Spirit*. London: Hodder & Stoughton, 1982; page 44.)

If we can achieve the truly childlike attitude of absolute trust in our heavenly Father, we can express our living faith in his good promises and generous gifts by using a tongue of adoration and praise. It is then a love language such as that known between a mother and her baby before the complication and inhibition of 'formal' language develops.

Perhaps of all the gifts, handling the gift of tongues in a small group raises the most queries. Paul gives advice for the exercise of discipline and control, as he does for the gift of prophecy: 'If anyone speaks in a tongue, two – or at the most three – should speak, one at a time, and someone must interpret' (1 Corinthians 14:27). Some wonder at this sense of human control, especially of a gift that is associated with ecstatic experiences of the Spirit. The fact of the matter is that because part of the fruit of the Spirit is 'self-control' (Galatians 5:23), anyone who is ministering in the Spirit is not uncontrolled, but is *more* self-controlled. The truly Spirit-filled person shows self-discipline, and readily subjects to discipline in the fellowship of the church. A great sense of inner joy and peace may accompany such ministry, but there should not be disorder and confusion, 'for God is not a God of disorder but of peace' (1 Corinthians 14:33).

Sometimes it is the fear of things getting out of control that hinders our childlike trust and prevents us moving in the Spirit. A respected leader in our church was struggling with the new life in the Spirit that was beginning to manifest in our church groups. After a sermon I had preached on the text, 'do not worry about tomorrow, for tomorrow will worry about itself. Each day has enough trouble of its own' (Matthew 6:34), he stopped me on the way out of church. 'You know,' he said, 'I'm not troubled at all about what has happened so far. I'm worried only about what might happen in the future.' I had to say to him that not only was he not trusting my leadership, but he was not trusting God's care and control of our situation. He needed to come to that new degree of childlike trust – something difficult for a senior, capable businessman – in order to find a new release of the Spirit in his own life.

Any small group will have members in that position – longing for new life personally, but needing time to work out, in the light of scripture, their own response to what God is doing. It took months for me to be fully open to the gifts of the Spirit, to believe that they are gifts for the church today and therefore for my life as well. I was particularly anxious not to judge Scripture in the light of the new experiences to which sincere Christians testified, but rather to understand the movement and gifts of the Spirit in the light of all that I had been taught from Scripture.

Somehow the gift of tongues was the key issue to be sorted out.

Nowadays it is quite normal to assume that a number of Christians in any small group may have the gift of tongues. Indeed, in our own fellowship the subject would seldom be talked about, since it would be assumed that through basic biblical teaching following conversion, the gifts of the Spirit would have been well covered, and any personal queries or difficulties would have been dealt with through one-to-one counselling. The key thing in the small group is for individuals to move from private expression of the gift of tongues to its use in the corporate life of the group.

For this to happen the group needs instruction about the New Testament way of receiving the gift in the church:

- *It is to be exercised in an orderly way*, as we have seen from 1 Corinthians 14:27.
- *It is to be accompanied by interpretation*: 'someone must interpret' (1 Corinthians 14:27). The leader can assure the group that if no one else is there with the gift of interpretation, he himself will pray for the ability to interpret. Equally, in verse 13 we are told that, 'anyone who speaks in a tongue should pray that he may interpret what he says.' What is quite clear is that, 'if there is no interpreter, the speaker should keep quiet in the church and speak to himself and God' (v 28). In practice, it is seldom necessary to become over self-conscious in this matter. We are dealing with a gift of love, and with wise leadership the group soon grows confident in the expression of gifts.

  When the group is comfortable together, it will relax over the question of interpretation. If the tongue is given early on in the meeting, the interpretation may come later. Sometimes the full meaning is given through interventions from several people.

- *The need for discernment*. The group needs to discern (as with prophecy) between contributions that may be of self or from Satan, rather than from God. The selfish form of counterfeit tongues is often frenzied or forced. The Satanic tongue is usually uncontrolled and unpleasantly gutteral, and is often accompanied by a sense of coldness, or of darkness or fear in the more sensitive members of the group. It can be authoritatively rebuked in the name of Jesus Christ.

- *Not everyone has the gift*. It must be understood that not everyone in the group should expect to have the gift of tongues. Paul makes this clear when he asks, 'Are all apostles? Are all prophets? Are all teachers? Do all work miracles? Do all have gifts of healing? Do all speak in tongues? Do all interpret?' (1 Corinthians 12:29–30.) The implied answer, indicated by the linguistic construction of this verse, is a firm 'no'. If everyone had exactly the same gifts that would be no 'body' made up of many different parts, each with its different function and purpose.

- *Sometimes the gift of tongues is expressed in singing*. This usually needs one or two fairly musical people who can help to develop the tongues singing around a simple chordal structure. If there is an instrumentalist, the group can be similarly helped by decorating a simple chord that holds the singing in tune. Such worship singing often leads to the release of some prophetic message or a word of knowledge, but is to be thought of as an extension of the individual's praise 'to God', and hardly requires formal 'interpretation'.

- *The use of silence*. It is important to allow silence after the expression of tongues. If he needs to, the leader can direct this so that it is purposeful and creative. Often the silence arises from a God-given sense of awe at being in his holy presence, and should not be broken by human intervention.

The implication of Paul's instructions in 1 Corinthians 14 is that only a few ever pray aloud in tongues, and the experience of many renewed groups is that tongues and interpretation happen *regularly* but not *always*. If the gift of tongues has not been expressed, that is no reason to feel that the group has not been 'in the Spirit'. However, Paul is firm in saying that if the gifts are there, they must be given out: 'my brothers, be eager to prophesy, and do not forbid speaking in tongues. But everything should be done in a fitting and orderly way' (1 Corinthians 14:39–40).

The power to know

Messages of knowledge and wisdom
In his list in 1 Corinthians 14:26, Paul speaks of these gifts being expressed when the church is gathered for worship, prayer and scriptural instruction. He refers to the gifts as a 'word of instruction' or a 'revelation'. In our own fellowship we received a string of such messages from God when we first met together to find his programme for our worship and witness in Harborne.

On one occasion the message God gave us led to a remarkable co-ordination of our prayer and pastoral work. My colleague and I were visiting a man in the parish who was suffering from a terminal illness. He was opening up his life to the gospel and we were encouraged by our visits. Sadly, at a critical stage of ministry, he lost rationality, so we brought his need to the praying group. We waited in silence for God's instructions. 'I believe we are called to pray that until that man dies, whenever the clergy visit they will coincide with his few moments of rationality,' someone said. We prayed the prayer, and for the remaining weeks of his life it was always answered. But we had another problem: his wife refused us access to him. Again, we brought this new situation to our praying group. 'I believe we are called to pray that woman out of the way,' the same person said, with a degree of vehemence that took us all by surprise. Amazingly, and unexpectedly, the man's wife took a job and installed a full-time nurse in the home, who allowed us regular access, until that man died in faith. Only after his death did we learn a family secret which had been hidden from us through all the months of our contact with the family. There was a younger daughter, who was a Christian missionary abroad. She had prayed daily for her father, over many years, without any of us in the church knowing about her. When she came home for the funeral she was so thrilled to hear our side of the story, and we were delighted to see that God's messages to us were as much an answer to her prayers as they were to ours. The 'message of knowledge' was vital to us pastorally, so that we could know the degree of persistence we were called to show in gospel ministry, and so that we could relate the ministry of the spiritually gifted praying group to the everyday work of pastoral care and witness.

Clearly these particular gifts are not always expressed in a worship meeting. Often they are vital in group counselling, especially when a person has blocked off some past, painful experience, and we need discernment for the next stage of prayer ministry. On one occasion a woman was referred to us for prayer counsel from a nearby mental hospital. The psychiatrist felt that her problem was a deeply spiritual one. At our very first meeting I was aware that there was a sexual problem, almost certainly due to child abuse. She however, denied this and presented her difficulty entirely in terms of regular occult practice, which had brought her to a position of complete disorientation. She was counselled to join us regularly for worship and prayer. A small group was established to pray for her regularly and to be available at any hour of day or night for ministry. But things grew worse rather than better. Eventually, we asked that she should be willing to share her problem with the whole 'Open to God' praying group, which at that stage was some 120 people. She was willing for this, so everyone took her needs home for ongoing private prayer. In the middle of the night, one of our elders woke up with the thought, 'She's been assaulted.' He related this in his mind to this woman's prayer need. When he shared this insight with me I assured him that we had already questioned her firmly along that line, but she had denied any wrong sexual activity. However, we agreed to confront her again. When we did so, she replied, 'Oh yes, from the ages of nine to sixteen I was regularly assaulted by the men who slept with my mum. We all shared the same bedroom.' After that confession, we were ready for the next stage of prayer ministry, which led to notable deliverance from her troubles.

Such a story is a confession of failure and stupidity on my part, and yet, because of the way it happened, we were helped to learn more about God's way of working: We began to understand the role of different groups, both small and large, and we saw the importance of the message of knowledge being given at the moment of need. We understood more of the sovereignty of God's timing in bringing all the elements of need together, and resolving them as the gifts of the Spirit were exercised.

These message gifts are to be used in the ministry of personal counselling but they are also given for the decision-making processes of the elders, Standing Committee, Church Council and all the other planning groups that organise the life of the church – from the finance team through to the missionary group and the youth workers. All these committees or sub-committees are themselves vital small groups where Holy Spirit gifts need to be exercised. Some who speak words of wisdom or knowledge in these planning bodies may not be very conscious of the divine origin of their words. However, others in the church will recognise that advice from certain people always registers with a supernatural impact, and through their words the Holy Spirit guides the church into wise decisions. Such people may also have a reputation for being naturally wise and knowledgeable. It is not surprising that God's Spirit speaks particularly with messages of knowledge and wisdom through those who are skilled in giving just the right words in their everyday relationships.

Of course, there are those with such gifts who are not necessarily on the decision-making bodies of the church. To enable their voices to be heard and their gifts to be expressed, we have periodic times of calling the whole church together for a sequence of daily prayer times when we can wait upon God and hear his voice speaking to us. We do this particularly when we are planning special evangelistic or missionary projects, when we feel called to change the existing structures of church life, or when we undertake a major building programme. Time and again we have been given God's go-ahead through a word of wisdom supplied from a quite unexpected source in the congregation. The word is then weighed and considered by those called to make the final decisions, and the details are worked out through the normal processes of human planning. However, once God's voice has been heard, the planning group has the backing of the whole fellowship, both in prayer and in practical terms of finance and commitment to a programme of events.

Distinguishing between spirits

Since Satan is described as appearing to be 'an angel of light', and is known as 'the deceiver', we always have to beware lest he intrudes through the attitudes, actions or the spoken contributions of church members. This is, of course, true of the wider church as well as of the small group. His opportunity may seem greater in a home group, though, especially where the leaders are inexperienced. Furthermore, the greater depth of fellowship that can be experienced in the smaller group means that people are often more trusting and relaxed with each other, and are not on guard against satanic intrusion. Consequently, they are often caught unawares.

A colleague of mine had a clear gift of discerning spirits and would frequently say 'That's the wrong spirit.' Immediately we were aware that a Christian brother or sister was being subtly used by the enemy, and we could take action accordingly. Sometimes a gentle rebuke or correction would be required, and one of the elders would take the person aside and speak in a careful and loving manner in order to correct the fault. As in dealing with obvious sin, we always remember Galatians 6:1, 'If someone is caught in a sin, you who are spiritual should restore him gently.' I do not suggest that in a serious matter this is handled by a home group leader, although questions of minor disagreement may be dealt with at that level.

It is never easy when the wrong spirit is at work to distinguish between that which is directly Satan's working and that which is sinful human choice. But there are certain guidelines:

The Lordship of Jesus is denied

In doctrinal matters, the evil spirit will always deny Christ's lordship. 'No one can say "Jesus is Lord", except by the Holy Spirit' (1 Corinthians 12:3).

A young woman frequently caused a disturbance in our Bible study and prayer groups. Time and again friends sought to love her and care for her, and the clergy ministered to her and tried to bring order to her life. She was adamant in her unwillingness to go Christ's way and would not cease her disturbing and disruptive behaviour. In the end she revealed her true position, in what proved to be a final attempt to offer her friendship and fellowship. I had planned to meet her in a public place in the centre of Birmingham, since it was unwise for any clergyman to see her alone in a private place, and as soon as I arrived for the interview she began cursing Christ and vehemently denied that he is Lord and God. None of us could help her any further at that stage. Our previous discernment was confirmed and the fellowship had to be protected from her influence.

John calls attention to this doctrinal test in his second epistle, and warns us to watch out for deceivers. 'Many deceivers, who do not acknowledge Jesus Christ as coming in the flesh, have gone out into the world. Any such person is the deceiver and the antichrist' (2 John 7). He is adamant in warning us to reject false teachers, 'If anyone comes to you and does not bring this teaching, do not take him into your home or welcome him. Anyone who welcomes him shares in his wicked work' (vs 10–11).

We have known such false teachers to infiltrate our groups, claiming at first to be orthodox in their beliefs but eventually proving to be from an occult background. Paul describes such opponents of the truth: 'They are the kind who worm their way into homes and gain control over weak-willed women, who are loaded down with sin and swayed by all kinds of evil desires, always learning but never able to acknowledge the truth' (2 Timothy 3:6–7). In our experience, such people trouble weak-willed men as much as 'weak-willed women'. The fact is that such deceivers always go for weak and vulnerable people whom they can dominate and rule.

Disunity

The power-seeking person is often used by Satan to bring disunity to a group. The way of God's Spirit is always the way of love. Every version of false religion works on a power basis instead of a love basis. In the wider church such people seek to put themselves forward for key positions where they can exert influence and power. In the smaller gathering they can often cause dissension by complaining about the leadership of the group and creating a general sense of dissatisfaction among the members. If, under such pressures, the leaders stand down, they then offer themselves in the leadership role.

The person with the gift of distinguishing between spirits will always pick up the pride and arrogance that lies behind such moves, and will know it is always Satan's ploy to attack Christian leaders, at every level of church life.

Accusation

Some are used by the enemy to bring a sense of accusation against the members of the group. We have seen that the Holy Spirit through his words always brings comfort and encouragement. Of course, there may well be occasions for correction and reproof, but that is expressed by the leadership of the church. It is their specific responsibility in oversight to care for the church and, under God, to exercise discipline. The sort of accusation I refer to is brought by the rather needy and frustrated person who becomes a self-appointed prophet or prophetess, always calling the group to order with sharp words demanding repentance, and constantly castigating both the small group and the wider church for its ineffectiveness. Such accusation is doing the work of the 'accuser of the brethren' for him, and the damage it causes is readily discerned as the work of the evil one.

In any case, such preoccupation with sin and the need for repentance easily takes our eyes away from God and his forgiving love for us. It can lead a small group into a hypochondriacal type of pseudo-spirituality. Philip Toynbee has a searching comment in his autobiographical journal, *Part of a Journey*: 'Repentance, Penitence, Contrition – these are all good words, but haven't they come to imply a rather grandiose obsession with our own sinful selves? One chic notion is that the past must be continuously scoured by confession.' (London: Collins, 1981; page 20.) Obviously, any group of Christians should repent of known sin, but it should never be preoccupied with sin and confession rather than with the Lord himself. It should, rather, be trusting him, loving him and obeying him. We are not to do the devil's work in mutual accusation, but rather seek God's will and do it gladly together.

Sometimes the enemy tries to wreak havoc in a group through sickness which is linked to spiritual warfare in which the group is engaged. I was once called to pray with a vicar and his wife who were working in a part of Birmingham that was difficult to penetrate spiritually. It emerged that for more than three years the wife had become so ill on the day of their main prayer time, that she had seldom managed to get to the meeting. They had treated this as normal sickness, had sought medical help and had taken the prescribed medicines. Then it suddenly dawned on them that this was part of Satan's tactics to weaken the small praying nucleus of the church. As I knew something of the history of spiritual warfare in that parish, and the pattern of attack on previous vicars, it was an obvious thing to deal with the sickness by a prayer for deliverance. It was one of those occasions when one rather glibly testifies, 'I prayed, and the recurrent sickness stopped completely!' Of course, in deliverance prayer it is not always as simple as that. There may be a physical or psychological illness that needs the appropriate treatment, or some other point of spiritual bondage may need to be discerned and dealt with.

Such an occurrence shows how critical it is to use the Holy Spirit gifts in spiritual warfare. That couple could have sought other forms of healing, and would have done so in vain since the fundamental grip of evil had to be discerned and broken.

Not all discernment comes as a flash of divine disclosure. In this instance I already knew something of the background of the church's life, in which the couple served, and this knowledge helped considerably in concluding that it was reasonable to assume direct Satanic attack on the ministry of that church. At other times a direct revelation of information, that could not be gained other than by the Holy Spirit's intervention, is vital in order to discern the root of the enemy attack.

At the National Evangelical Anglican Clergy (NEAC) conference at Caister in May 1988, a group met for a workshop on Deliverance Ministry. During the final session we all ministered to each other in a time of worship and prayer. One clergyman shared some of the battle in his own parish, and as a group we waited on God. Several pictures were given, one of which described a major explosion, which at first the group did not know how to interpret. Then the vicar himself told us that his church had been on the site of a munitions factory which had been totally destroyed in a major explosion. The person who had the discernment did not have this information, but he pointed us to the root cause of conflict in that place. It was a community that had once been destroyed by the violence of weapons of warfare, the production of which had previously sustained its life. It was an area that had experienced widespread griefs and sorrows, some of which had not been resolved and healed even to that day. As he was given other comforting words this vicar went home with the sure knowledge that God's good hand was upon his parish, and that his healing was at hand.

Thus the right use of past experience and of human knowledge, and the direct intervention of God by his Spirit in revelation, both combine for this ministry of distinguishing between spirits. The insight that God gives to us directly is, of course, vital in cases of demonic affliction, since this is usually totally hidden from the sufferer. A worshipper in the synagogue at Capernaum (Mark 1:21–28) had been troubled by an unclean spirit without his need of deliverance being noticed by anyone. It was not until Jesus came along and, by his holy presence, confronted the evil spirit, that the need was brought to light and the man delivered.

The power to do

Healing

The power to 'do' relates to the 'gifts of healing' (1 Corinthians 12:9) and 'miraculous powers' (12:10). Notice that the ability to heal is described in plural terms: 'gifts of healing'. We could, perhaps, translate the phrase more accurately by saying 'gifts of healings'. The implication of this is that healing is not normally to be exercised by one outstandingly gifted person in the church. Nowhere do we find in the New Testament the touring, crusading evangelist, whose ministry is heralded by placards and promises of healing sessions in the crusade meetings. Rather, healing happens from time to time, here and there. Sometimes it is done by the apostles Peter and Paul. Sometimes by Philip the deacon. On one occasion it happens on the way to a worship service in the temple. At another time it is, indeed, part of an evangelistic campaign.

The clear lesson for the church today is that everyone in the body of Christ might hope to be used in this way. But because God is sovereign in the allocation of his gifts, and gives 'just as he determines' (1 Corinthians 12:11), and because it is essential to the concept of the body of Christ that not all the members have the same gift, it is unlikely, indeed unthinkable, that everyone who hopes to be used in healing will find themselves gifted in the ministry. John Wimber describes how in his church 'the people are taking healing and other supernatural gifts to the streets, leading many who otherwise would not be open to the message of the gospel of Christ. I estimate that twenty per cent of our people regularly see someone healed through their prayers. The gifts are not confined to church services; they are tools employed in reaching the lost.' (*Power Evangelism*, by John Wimber with Kevin Springer. London: Hodder & Stoughton; page 55.) The implication of this passage is that eighty per cent do not see healing gifts expressed as part of their ministry, and that makes biblical sense. They are still part of the ministry team of the church, they no doubt witness and pray in a believing way, but others are used with their healing gifts to bring God's work to completion. In our own fellowship we value the gifts and insights of doctors and other medical workers as much as any gifts of spiritual healing.

The indisputable factor for us is to minister in small groups. In Chapter 6 I describe how this can be done with a group of elders in the church. But even before people seek the prayer ministry of the elders, they will normally have been prayed for and counselled by a small group who unite in bonds of prayer and concern for the needy person. Often there is the release of healing or deliverance gifts at this stage in the proceedings, but in some cases the breakthrough comes as the elders, together with those already engaged in healing prayer, unite in ministry within the context of a communion service.

Within this pattern of shared ministry some will grow in confidence and will begin to wonder if they have a gift of healing. They realise that others seek them out for help and prayer, and time after time healing prayer is answered in a notable way. They will be conscious of a tingling sensation in their hands as they pray or perhaps a fragrant aroma arising from the person for whom they pray. Extremes of heat may be felt and the one prayed for may break into a sweat. We should not be surprised at a sensation of warmth when the 'fire' falls. Many people comment that we do not normally expect 'tongues of fire' (Acts 2: 3) as on the day of Pentecost when the Holy Spirit comes to an individual, but in the healing ministry a sense of warmth is not at all uncommon as God's Spirit touches a person at the point of need. Both are signs to help us discern, from an outward happening, the inward working of grace. Those who are called to minister in this way find a strong desire to intercede for sick friends, and find themselves driven to read literature and seek instruction about the healing ministry.

It is at this point that careful leadership must nurture a developing ministry. If it is not exercised within the fellowship of the local church, the person concerned may become dissatisfied and turn to one of the many parachurch healing organisations that abound these days. While there is obviously a place for such organisations, some of them become so preoccupied with one style of healing ministry that they become eccentric and sometimes positively unhelpful. Within a local church, healing is just one aspect of ministry and represents just one of the Spirit's gifts, so that the danger of imbalance is far less.

Healing gifts may emerge in the first instance within a home group. Home group leaders as well as ministers and elders of a church need to be encouraged to develop such ministries within their small group. Some people, of course, claim healing gifts in order to be in the limelight, and such immature behaviour must be discerned. The test which is consistently reliable is that a person with a genuine healing gift from God never pushes himself or herself forward, but always finds that others are taking the initiative in asking for help. Considerable damage can be done by those who make false claims to spiritual gifts. If ministry is forced upon needy people without gift and without authorisation by the leadership of the church, those who are prayed for lose faith in God's ability to heal, because nothing ever happens to them. They do not improve – indeed their condition worsens as they lose trust in God's power and in the ministry of those who claim an ability to pray for healing.

This sort of problem emerges most commonly in small groups in a church where leadership is devolved. Unless the leader of the small group is aware of the danger of some of his group claiming more ability and skill than they actually possess, it is unlikely that a minister or elder will be fully aware of what is going on. The healing ministry must be expressed within the mainstream life of a local church and not be a fringe activity that is practised without control and oversight. Of course, no one can stop well-meaning Christians praying for others in need. I am speaking of a person who makes blatant, unauthorised claims to have a gift of healing, and is acting on those claims without the recognition and goodwill of the leadership of the church.

There are so many excellent books on the healing ministry that I will only emphasise certain matters that are fundamental in expressing this gift in the life of a local church.

Repentance

Healing prayer is often offered without any examination of a person's life, and without dealing with aspects of past or current sin for which there must be repentance. We cannot help someone to believe God's promises of healing if there is no change of heart and mind towards him.

Deliverance

Just as personal responsibility for wrong-doing must be admitted, so any points of satanic bondage must be perceived. This could have come about because of someone's curse or evil prayer wish, or because of occult dabbling, or even because in the search for healing the needy person has consulted a spiritulist healing medium. If there has been such involvement, a deliverance prayer is vital as part of the healing ministry, and gifts of discernment will be exercised.

Sovereignty of timing

Sometimes healing is a progressive matter within the sovereignty of God's dealing with our lives. Desperate people want instant results, but there can be a wider purpose of grace which asks us to add patience to our faith.

I have been seriously ill on three different occasions, and looking back I can see God's overwhelming love in the timing of all the events surrounding hospitalisation and recuperation, both at a personal and family level. If anyone had attempted to short-circuit God's plans by achieving some instant healing ahead of God's time, many lessons important for my life and ministry would not have been learnt. I was at a meeting of ministers in Birmingham when Dr Alan Redpath, who suffered a massive stroke from which he was subsequently miraculously healed, testified to the same truth. He was momentarily almost angry when a person who had never experienced long-term illness, suggested that God's plan was always and only, quick and easy healing. 'We all have deep lessons to learn about God's love when we are laid aside in long-term illness,' he replied.

Persistent love

The ministry of the caring group is important not just for the group members to provide mutual support for each other, but also in order that the sick person can have a network of caring people on whom he or she can call. This is particularly true when a church grows so large that the leading pastors have insufficient time to give adequate ongoing counselling. The work has to be shared out in the wider community of love.

Focus on the cross

Healing in Bible terms is a much broader word than many think. It is linked to the concept of salvation and speaks of the total well-being that God's forgiveness brings to our lives. When Jesus spoke to the woman who was constantly haemorrhaging, and he knew that power had gone out of him for the healing of her illness, he said, 'Daughter, your faith has healed you' (Mark 5:34). Other versions translate this, 'your faith has saved you'. We can never minister physical or emotional healing in a way that divides up the human being into separate fragments. We must always pray for full salvation to be administered to the whole person, and in doing so must enable the one for whom we are praying to find their wholeness through Christ's work on the cross. There is a tendency today, as we are more fully aware of the gifts and power of the Spirit for healing through the ministry of the body of Christ, to forget that behind the release of the Spirit is the sacrifice of Christ for our sins, and that it is 'by his wounds we are healed' (Isaiah 53:5).

Miraculous powers

Because Paul speaks of 'miraculous powers' in the plural, like 'healings', he gives the impression that he is referring in very general terms to the power of God being released in the church. Those who express these gifts are thus to be channels for God's power rather than dominating figureheads in the church, renowned for miracles and healing. The gifts make *God* prominent in his church, not people.

Signs and wonders were, of course, characteristic of the ministry of Jesus. He raised the dead, drove out demons and performed nature miracles, and he promised his followers, 'anyone who has faith in me will do what I have been doing. He will do even greater things than these, because I am going to the Father' (John 14:12). The early church claimed this promise when it encountered serious opposition to gospel ministry, and God performed signs and wonders among his people. They prayed, 'Now, Lord, consider their threats and enable your servants to speak your word with great boldness. Stretch out your hand to heal and perform miraculous signs and wonders through the name of your holy servant Jesus' (Acts 4:29–30). Mighty works were also released when the Holy Spirit was poured out. They were seen in the ministry of the apostles. They raised the dead (Acts 9:36–42; 20:7–12), cast out evil spirits (Acts 16:18; 19:12) and performed nature miracles (Acts 16:26; 28:3–6). We read that 'God did extraordinary miracles through Paul' (Acts 19:11). This miracle-working power was at the heart of the growth of the early church, and by the Spirit of God the same power is available today. This is particularly the testimony of those engaged in 'power evangelism', inspired by the ministry of John Wimber and the Vineyard Fellowship. Wimber claims that the early church did not grow through preaching alone, but through miracle-working power accompanying the preaching and testimony of the disciples. 'Signs and wonders occurred fourteen times in the book of Acts in conjunction with preaching, resulting in church growth. Further, on twenty occasions church growth was a direct result of signs and wonders performed by the disciples. Rarely was church growth attributed to preaching alone.' (*Power Evangelism*, page 117.)

But miraculous powers were not exercised only by Jesus and the apostles. As Wimber says, 'more than the twelve healed the sick, cast out demons, experienced visions. Other Christians did. Signs and wonders were a part of daily life, expected by the church. Paul, Stephen, Cornelius, Ananias – none of them the original twelve – all practised signs and wonders.' (*Power Evangelism*, page 117.) Clearly the gift of 'miraculous powers' is released generally in the church, in that it is listed with all the other gifts for the body of Christ. It is not limited to the leadership or to super-spiritual members of the community. But that does mean that it must be used within the discipline of the local church. In our fellowship we would be suspicious of self-professed wonder-workers, because this is an area of ministry in the church where the immature person seeking fame and notoriety can easily push himself forward. Simon the sorcerer did so in Samaria, and incurred the wrath of Peter (Acts 8). The genuine, spiritually-minded person will always wait humbly to express his gifts, and will never minister in order to obtain any kind of personal reward, whether it be money or reputation. Also, a Christian with a notable ministry will always be recommended by trustworthy leaders from his previous church connection.

This will always be the test of a true, Spirit-gifted person. He will gladly join a small group in the church to which he has been called, and will serve humbly as a member of that fellowship. He will minister as God gives opportunity, and if there is an obvious gift of miraculous powers it will be clearly recognised by others who belong to the group.

We find that such ministry is not often experienced in the

regular home group meeting. This is because we have established a network of trained counsellors who look to God for the miracle of his healing power to be released as they pray in his name. Those with gifts in this direction tend to operate within this set-up and under its leadership, and those with a need for prayer and counsel tend to call on members of the counselling team for help. This means that any ministry involving the gift of miraculous powers takes place with the knowledge and supervision of the elders who lead and train the counselling group. It may take place in the context of a main Sunday service, or among the large number of worshippers gathered at an 'Open to God' mid-week meeting, or at an elders' healing communion service.

When the ministry is exercised at a larger meeting, the prayer and worship of the assembled company creates an atmosphere of God-centred praise which is enormously helpful to the teams of prayer counsellors. The choir is often used to lead worship as the ministry proceeds and, time and again, exactly the right words in the worship songs coincide with the prayer that is being offered in ministry.

We do not often observe the miracle happening there and then. We are called to pray and then believe that God will act to transform the situation, in his own time and way. During a meeting in Denmark, where our choir was on tour, the singers led a time of praise and worship and the clergy and other leaders were ministering to those who asked for prayer. A couple brought their five-year-old son whose foot had been twisted back on itself since birth, so that it was facing in the wrong direction. None of us who prayed for the lad would have claimed the gift of miraculous powers, but we prayed believing, and committed him to God's mercy. We left that church and returned to our base in Roskilde without seeing a miracle performed. However, we were told the next day that the foot had turned right round and the boy was walking normally for the first time.

Although John Wimber teaches that signs and wonders are a vital factor in bringing people to faith, as the word of God is preached, this is not always the case. During a BBC 2 interview for Pamela Armstrong's afternoon programme, it was my privilege to meet a lady who had not walked for nearly eighteen years and who suddenly heard a voice that she believed to be the voice of the Lord. He told her to get up out of her wheelchair and her straitjacket, and walk. This she did, to the amazement of her husband and children. What was more, although she had been reduced to surviving on a liquid diet for years, she was immediately able to eat again and it was clear that her whole digestive system had been made whole at the same time. However, although the lady attributed her healing to a miracle of God, the event did not change her husband's attitude at all. As I spoke with him he remained rooted in unbelief. The miracle of new birth may yet come to him and his wife's dramatic healing may yet speak to his life, but when I met him that mighty work of God had not brought him to faith.

For us, the miracles are God's 'plus'. Many people are brought to church and hear the gospel, as Christians testify of God's miracle-working power. But this testimony is not shouted from the house tops all the time, mainly because the enemy counter-attacks powerfully against any claim that Christ has won back someone who was formerly gripped in Satan's power. We prefer to wait for the evidence to emerge, for the new life to be seen, for the fruit of God's working to be manifested in a changed lifestyle. We do not assume that such happenings are the everyday norm of local church life, even though miracles were clearly a factor in the life of the early church. Sometimes we know of miraculous happenings taking place every day for weeks on end. Then it seems that we are given a quieter period. The previous work is consolidated as people receive ongoing counsel, and there is time to deal with normal duties and responsibilities.

It can be regarded by some as an unspiritual thing to say, but there is need for a rhythm of life and for the normality that enables a Christian fellowship to be faithful in small things. Some take the view that miracles should happen all the time. Quiet days of lowly service and care are seen as a sub-normal expression of powerful Christian life and ministry. However, in the natural creation there are surges of activity and quiet periods of consolidation ready for the next stage of growth. It can be so in the spiritual life too.

In the small group, whether it is a home group or the small

ministering group of counsellors, the insensitive individual who presses for daily miracles can bring enormous pressure on the leaders and other members of the group. Satan knows how to make us discouraged in God's work, and can often use such a person within the Christian fellowship to create a false expectation of miracle-working. The biblical evidence is that God moves in spectacular and supernatural ways at significant points in the history of his people. We note miracles at the time of the Hebrew people's exodus from Egypt, at the time of apostasy in the ministry of Elijah and Elisha, at the time of captivity in Babylon, and notably, of course, in the ministry of Jesus and following the outpouring of the Holy Spirit at Pentecost. Outbreaks of miracle-working have occurred in the history of the church at times of revival, and the rediscovery of faith for receiving supernatural Holy Spirit gifts is a characteristic of twentieth-century church renewal. However, it is not helpful for every church group to be pressurised by enthusiasts who consider that miraculous powers should be looked for all the time. This is a matter of God's sovereignty. We must live expectantly but not insistently.

As with other gifts we should expect to find that, at moments of special need and when we are desperate for the release of God's power because we are helpless without him, then God will act. The point of being together in the small group is that within the intimacy of our friendship in Christ, we can encourage one another to believe God for miraculous powers, when needed, and to join together in mutual service and care when that is the priority. What we need is wisdom for the exercise of spiritual gifts. Arnold Bittlinger links the working of miracles with God's gift of wisdom: 'The gift of working miracles has something in common with the word of wisdom. As a rule, there is a dangerous situation, then the mighty deed happens, and the result is that the danger is averted. In the case of the word of wisdom, the danger is usually of a spiritual nature, and only indirectly is life endangered, whereas the situation that calls for the working of a miracle usually involves the physical and a direct threat to body and life.' (Arnold Bittlinger, *Gifts and Graces*, London: Hodder & Stoughton 1967; page 41.) In conclusion we can say that these special gifts of extraordinary powers are for ordinary people for particular situations. Thus we see them as the generous provision of God for the fulfilling of the general commission of Christ in sending his disciples into the world. Bittlinger quotes from Joseph Brosch, confirming this: 'From every place to which messengers of Christ went, reports came back of how they had been granted the gift of miracles. It was in keeping with the promise Christ made when he gave the Great Commission, that one of the criteria in the expansion of the early church was that she should move forward in Spirit and power. If the tools God had chosen for the proclamation of the good news were lowly, then all the more could he accomplish mighty deeds with his tools and so make foolish the wisdom of the world.' (*Gifts and Graces*, page 41.)

5
Practical
leadership

Goals

To be effective, a group leader needs to be clear about the goal
he or she is trying to help the group achieve, and needs to be
able to communicate the goal, and a sense of vision for it, to the
group members. The goals we set, and the chance we stand of
achieving them, depend to a large extent on the size and nature
of the group. The two main group sizes we work with at St John's
are the small home group, and the intermediate community group
which is made up of three or four home groups meeting together.

Growing in Christlikeness
The ultimate goal for those meeting in small groups in a church
is to grow more like Jesus Christ in character and in ministry.
The purpose of God's gifts of ministry in the church is that 'we
all reach unity in the faith and in the knowledge of the Son of
God and become mature, attaining the whole measure of the
fulness of Christ' (Ephesians 4:13). This is why God gave 'some
to be apostles, some to be prophets, some to be evangelists, and
some to be pastors and teachers' (v 11). In the first instance the
people of God are trained 'for works of service, so that the body
of Christ may be built up' (v 12), but the ultimate purpose of
gifted ministry is to make people mature and Christ-like.

A home group leader may find this a daunting prospect. But

so does everyone called to the ordained ministry. The fact is that ministry is never exercised in isolation. It is always performed within and from the body of Christ, whether that is represented by the whole company of a local church, or by a small group that is part of the wider fellowship. If the task seems too difficult, the home group leader should stand down at once. There is no shame in being honest in saying that there is no real call to such heavy responsibility in the church. It is always better to minister well as a member of a flourishing group, than to lead badly so that others cannot exercise their ministries effectively. The same realism is required of the ordained minister of the gospel. It would be better for some to stand down than to persist in a task for which they do not have God's gift. This is a hard thing to do after years of agonising over a possible call to the ordained ministry and further years of costly training. But it would be far better for some to be usefully employed in God's service as lay people, than strive unsuccessfully in full-time preaching and pastoral work. If a call from God is wrongly perceived and a person is mistakenly ordained, the loss to the church of their valid ministry as a lay person is as significant as the damage that might be done by their incompetence in the ordained role. The value of small groups in a church is that they provide spheres for loving, fulfilling lay ministries to be exercised.

To achieve the goal of Christlikeness, the whole membership needs the home group as a place for learning to do 'works of service, so that the body of Christ may be built up' (Ephesians 4:12). The leader must therefore have a forward plan and vision to bring this about, seeing the potential for growth to maturity in Christ, both individually and corporately. At St John's we suggest this involves the following:

- analysing what is being achieved as any particular meeting progresses, ready to intervene with gentle correction if the sense of purpose gets lost.
- watching out for new members, or shy members, so that they do not get left behind in obtuse discussion or are left out as people form their natural friendship groups over coffee.

- seeking to be aware of all that the Father is doing in the little segment of his family represented by this group, and planning the overall programme accordingly, ensuring that, so far as possible, God's will is done.
- watching out for points of tension in the group and dealing with them as lovingly as possible.
- encouraging the right balance between the varying elements of the 'Open to God' style gathering, as already described.

If the leader has any queries the elders in overall charge of home groups can be consulted at any time. We find it is much easier for the initiative to come this way round. There is no sense in which the elders want to act as inspectors or supervisors, so they prefer a low-key presence, with constant availability for help and advice if it is asked for. Equally, some issues may be best raised with other home group leaders in the context of the community group, whose leader is regularly in consultation with the elders.

Kingdom outreach

When Jesus wanted to reach out to a wide number of people in a given geographical area, he sent out a group of seventy or so disciples (eg Luke 10) to do so. A group larger than that of the home group is still often best for this task of 'Kingdom outreach'. The 'community group' is the intermediate size of group which fills the gap in a larger church between the small home group and the large Sunday congregations. It is formed by a number of home groups meeting together regularly. The size of such 'intermediate' groups will, of course, vary from church to church, according to the overall size of the Sunday congregation and the number of home groups in existence.

When such groups meet, the programme may be essentially the same as for the smaller home group, in terms of worship, prayer, praise, testimony and ministry. The added dimension is the possibility of a greater number of church members getting to know one another in a relationship of love and trust. This is especially so if they work together in some form of Kingdom outreach – perhaps planning and producing evangelistic events, undertaking diocesan or inter-church tasks or resourcing areas of need in the wider ministry of the church.

Building community

Other community groups may find that their main goal needs to be to develop a greater sense of community in the church fellowship. Three or four home groups can meet together for social purposes from time to time, without an ongoing spiritual programme. This can be just as important for the wider life of the church as a more task-oriented group. The aim is for more people in the larger congregation to come to know each other in a real and personal way. Too many church-goers have to be content with surreptitious chatter before a service begins, or a casual and superficial conversation on the way out of church, and they only belong with serious commitment to the handful of fellow Christians whom they know at a deeper level in their small home groups.

Enhancing communication

Leaders of the community groups can provide a useful link between home group leaders and the elders or ordained staff in the church. They can keep in regular touch with the elders and staff, and form an essential link in the chain of communication in a larger church. Communication becomes difficult when the number of home group leaders is so large that it is hardly ever possible for all of them to meet together on any one occasion. The art of local church leadership is to keep all the leaders of all small groups – home groups, youth groups, music and worship groups etc – informed and involved, so that all serve their God and their church with good will and common purpose. Too often, the small group develops its own momentum regardless of the call and goal of the wider church. Any scheme that aids communication among leaders is vitally important for the unity of the local church. Community groups with leaders responsible for a maximum of seventy or so in the congregation enhance this vital togetherness.

It is fair to say that it is not always easy to sustain additional regular meetings of this intermediate-sized grouping. Some who value the small home group are uncomfortable in the larger setting. Members are already used to looking to their own home group leader for oversight, and may not respond well to the leader of the community group. However, for the sake of a more effective programme of evangelism, wider fellowship and deeper unity, and better communication in the church, it is important to persist.

Geared for growth

Many churches do not attain their full potential for growth because their structures do not allow for all their members to be active in expressing ministry, love, and care to each other. Someone has suggested that a church can operate in one of three ways:

- like a gondola: one man propels the boat and the rest are passengers who pay the gondolier to do his job, working on their behalf;
- like a galley: each slave rows hard at the cracking of a whip;
- like a galleon: crewed by a team, in which each person has his own job to do under the captain's leadership. The means of propulsion is the wind!

Any reading of the New Testament shows that although the early church was totally reliant on the strongly blowing Holy Spirit for its growth, the structures were carefully worked out by the apostles. The problem that we face today is that many mainstream churches have become heavily institutionalised, and an immense amount of effort is taken up keeping the cumbersome machinery of committees and synods on the move. Someone has likened the contemporary church to a puffing, straining, traction engine. Laboriously, but with magnificent dignity and enormous power, it moves towards its destination – slowly! It is hugely admired, but manifestly out-dated; it is beautiful in an old-fashioned way, but it is an antique, geared for yesterday's conditions. In a rather sharp and critical description, Dr Clifford

Hill sums it up in *The Day Comes*, suggesting that the people of God, instead of being a living, spiritual organism, 'has become a giant organisation encumbered by institutionalism, crippled with materialism, struck dumb by unbelief, emaciated by division, enfeebled by spiritual impotence'.

If a local church is to get anywhere for God it needs to challenge institutionalism and form itself into groups which are themselves living organisms, moving at the direction of God himself as each one grows in the love of the Spirit. Then the church could be seen no longer as a chunking piece of outmoded machinery, irrelevant to contemporary needs, but a living body of love, inspired and guided by the Spirit of God, to serve the needs of the world in which it is set.

For small groups in the church to fulfil this purpose, there must not only be a clear goal for them but a carefully devised programme of worship, learning, prayer and fellowship so that group members become the living body that God can use within the wider church. The following section represents a summary of some of the issues already considered, so that a group leader can take his or her group forward – growing in love and trust, in mutual ministry and obedience to God's will. It represents a series of 'handy hints for home group leaders' and might be thought of as a 'Handbook for Small Group Leadership'. One of the difficulties when large numbers in a congregation assume leadership roles is that it is hard to ensure that all have caught the same vision. Group leaders hand over to others at different stages in the group's life. Some may only have experienced the group during a bad patch, perhaps with poor relationships and little joy in worship and prayer. Others may be unaware of all that God has revealed by his Spirit to the wider church in previous years. A pamphlet for home group leaders could be prepared on the basis of some of the insights presented here, and could be required reading for new leaders in your particular local church, as you incorporate issues that are important for you.

A certain repetitiveness at this stage is quite deliberate so that no points are missed in this leadership summary.

Leading the home group

Home groups are not intended to be merely prayer times or Bible study groups. They are meant to contain all the elements of the larger fellowship meeting – worship and praise, shared scripture and testimony, prayer and Bible exposition, fellowship and mutual ministry. The details and ideas given in this section will necessarily have to be varied from one church to another. The groups, leadership and social patterns will all be different for different churches. I have based the suggestions which follow on the structures and experience of St John's, Harborne.

Worship and praise

Maintain the emphasis on praise

It is the leader's responsibility to maintain an emphasis on worship and praise in the course of a normal home group evening programme. He or she should arrange for adequate musical leadership. Group members are frequently diffident about their musical ability. Sometimes I have known groups claim a total lack of musical talent, only to find at some later stage that several members had musical skills which they were too frightened to offer. It is the leader's task to encourage members to bring their musical instruments to meetings – even a single wind instrument can give a lead in worship singing.

Learn to wait on God

It is vital to train the group in learning how to wait upon God in an extended time of praise and worship. The temptation is for someone to intervene with an intercessory prayer, which immediately takes the emphasis away from God himself and focuses attention on human needs. Group members should always be encouraged to worship with Bibles open. As their minds feed on the scriptures they can respond to God with love and adoration. They can share the scriptures with others and choose appropriate hymns or worship songs for the developing theme of praise.

Move with the Spirit

It is important to ensure that the worship time does not deteriorate into an inconsequential sequence of favourite choruses, chosen at random. As a theme develops in the time of worship, the choice of songs should be governed by that theme and not by the personal preferences of the worshippers. It is all too easy to choose choruses which can be used as a psychological 'switch on', creating an artificial atmosphere of worship, which is man-centred rather than God-centred. The leader needs to help the group become sensitive to the leading of the Holy Spirit in the choice of hymns and worship songs. At any one point in a meeting there are few possible choices. Clearly, if it is the right moment to sing a quiet, meditative hymn about the cross, like 'When I survey the wondrous cross', it would not be right for a member of the group to choose a rousing song like 'Rejoice, rejoice, Christ is in you'. When a group is moving in the Spirit, there is tremendous sense of rightness in the sequence of songs, Scripture passages and words of encouragement, knowledge and prophecy.

In helping the group to expect such clear leading from the Spirit of God, the leader must be careful not to discourage inexperienced members. The demand for 'right' contributions can cause some to clam up, frightened to speak in case their words or their choice of song might be inappropriate for that moment. It must be made clear that no one need be worried about making a mistake. It is the leader's responsibility to steer the meeting back to the main theme of the evening through gentle intervention. It is far better for the occasional inappropriate contribution to be made than for the whole group to be inhibited and fearful of sharing.

Don't prolong worship artificially

The leader needs to be sensitive about the timing of various sections of a meeting. It is easy to overrun time in the opening worship period because of a desire to 'arrive'. There is often a climax point in praise where even a small group worshipping together can sense a degree of awe and reverence in the presence of God's holiness. All the members of the group bring to the meeting anxieties, troubles and worldly concerns. All come from secular duties, and it can take some time to adjust to God's presence. The leader, however, will be conscious of other priorities – the need to have adequate time for prayer and Bible study as well as having time to express true friendship and fellowship. The leader must therefore sense when the climax of praise has come, in order to bring discipline to the meeting and move it on to other things. It is such a good experience to spend time rejoicing in God, that many are tempted to do nothing else. Leadership brings direction and control to the worship time.

Shared Scripture

It is the sharing of Scripture verses and passages that enables a meeting to remain God-centred. This is particularly true, as we have seen, in the time of worship and praise. When a group is being led by the Spirit of God, it is as though God himself is preparing and presenting the most beautifully formed sermon or talk, using contributions from one person and another to put it together. In order for this to happen it is important that no individual wrongly dominates the meeting, putting his own thought forms upon the gathering and so preventing God's message from coming through. I was once leading a meeting at Ascension time, and turned to the last verses of Luke's Gospel. The thought in my mind was, 'power from on high' (Luke 24:49) and 'great joy' (v 52). But one of the group seized on the one word 'hands' from v 50: 'he lifted up his hands and blessed them'. Verses were shared from many different parts of the Bible, some of which I had never noticed before. Truths were shared and insights were given which could never have come from one human mind, and the result was that we were all open to what God wanted to say to us, rather than to the best thoughts of one human mind. That is not to decry the value of a well-prepared Bible exposition. It is simply to say that it is different from the experience of a variety of people all sharing from the Scriptures under the direct leading of God's Holy Spirit. Such corporate sharing brings a remarkable awareness of God's presence as he speaks to his people and raises the whole exercise to the level of expressing spiritual gifts. That is just how Paul urged Christians to work together: 'When you come together, everyone has a hymn, or a word of instruction, a revelation, a tongue or an interpretation' (1 Corinthians 14:26).

Spiritual gifts

From time to time the leader should openly encourage the expression of spiritual gifts. Newcomers need to know that they are free to give a word of knowledge or a prophecy, or that they are free to pray in tongues. The leader might choose to intervene after someone has prayed in tongues to encourage the group to wait upon God for an interpretation. Sometimes the interpretation will come through more than one person.

Some people receive their messages in pictoral form. Discernment is needed with such pictures, both on the part of the leader and the person who shares the picture. The leader must ensure that some do not use the opportunity for selfish display. It is possible that certain members of the group might form a habit of sharing pictures, without discerning whether they are truly from God. Any individual can be helped to test their own picture by praying to the Lord before it is shared. If the picture is black and accusing it could well be from Satan rather than from God. In prayer we can ask that if it comes from the Lord the picture will become even more clear and definite, and if it is from the enemy it will be taken away completely. Usually, if a picture is from God, the person who receives it will find himself deeply constrained to share it with the group. Sometimes someone may indicate after the meeting is over that he had a picture but was too bashful to speak it out. That person should be encouraged to share it at the next opportunity. If it is important for the group to hear the message, the leader could share it at the next meeting, even in the person's absence.

If a word of knowledge or a prophecy is given it is important that the leader should note the message and make sure it is tested by the group as a whole and then communicated to the church leadership. This can be done through the Community Group meeting. In considering what is spoken, it is wise to test the spirit in which the words are spoken. Sometimes an utterance can be made which carries a strong sense of condemnation, rebuke or even accusation. If a statement is strongly accusatory it is certainly more likely to be devilish than godly. Satan is the 'accuser of the brethren', and will readily use a Christian brother or sister to do his work for him. Equally, there may be the need for a right rebuke of wrong attitudes in the church. This, again, should be noted by the leader and reported back to the church as a whole.

Testimony

From time to time there should be space for testimony. The leader's task is to ensure that this is as God-centred as every other part of the meeting. The point of testimony is to 'declare the mighty acts of God'. It is to encourage a deeper fellowship and promote a deeper trust in the Father's love. As John expressed it, 'we proclaim to you what we have seen and heard, so that you also may have fellowship with us' (1 John 1:3). Some testimony positively *discourages* deeper fellowship! It is possible to speak of personal Christian experience in a proud way which discourages those who lack such a vivid experience of God in their own lives. The leader can prevent this happening by explaining beforehand the purpose of the testimony time and giving guidelines to those present.

It is unwise to draw out premature testimony from those who have been recently delivered from occult involvement. Such witness is particularly annoying to the enemy and often leads to powerful counter-attack. The same can happen if Christians give boastful accounts of the deliverance that others have received. When the disciples of Jesus returned from their ministry campaign when they first preached the kingdom, healed the sick, and cast out demons (Luke 10:17), Jesus said, 'Do not rejoice that the spirits submit to you, but rejoice that your names are written in heaven' (Luke 10:20). The eternal consequence of final salvation was of more importance than a limited demonstration of power over the evil one. Some missionary speakers telling of their exploits abroad are aware of this problem and will warn their hearers not to brag about stories of notable conversions, especially those involving deliverance from demonic powers. Such converts are vulnerable and need continuing care and prayer.

Nonetheless there is a place for testimony, especially from the new Christian. 'If you confess with your mouth, "Jesus is Lord", and believe in your heart that God raised him from the dead, you will be saved' (Romans 10:9). Not only is God glorified and the faith of other Christians stimulated, but the new convert grows by virtue of telling out the truth concerning God's working in his or her life.

Prayer

Intercession should flow naturally from the mutual love and care that the members of the group have for each other. It is easy for prayer in the small group to become very local and parochial – indeed, sometimes the requests are entirely limited to the narrow interests and personal and family needs of the group itself. The leader's responsibility is to be aware of the wider issues in the world and in the church at large, which should be brought before the Lord. It is disgraceful if Christians meet together for prayer and fail to intercede for headline issues. Sometimes the praying is very personal and pietistic because too little time has been allowed for intercession. In St John's 'Open to God' meeting the time given to intercession is often deliberately short, since the emphasis of this gathering is on the power of praise. An imbalance of time in what is primarily a praise meeting can reasonably be given to corporate worship. The same is not the case in the smaller group. There it is harder to achieve a satisfactory worship time and easier to engage in meaningful intercession.

Special prayer times and targets

The leader may want to encourage smaller groups within the main home group to meet separately for special prayer topics. Groups of two or three might pray together for friends and members of their families whom they are seeking to win for Christ. Others may plan to meet to pray for someone who is seriously ill or who needs ongoing deliverance prayer. Particular prayer topics for the church will be given at the Community Group meeting. It is also helpful to issue a monthly Prayer Diary for the use of every church member, perhaps listing an item for prayer for each day, and also the names of three or four church members. The electoral roll provides the most obvious source of names for the Prayer Diary.

The leaders need to beware lest the well-meaning desire to pray in smaller groups takes away from faith and expectation of answered prayer in the larger gathering. There is a form of pietism which needs to earn favour with God by an emphasis on personal prayer times at the expense of practical action. Thus, there will always be some who would rather stay at home to pray for a service of worship or an evangelistic meeting, when the duty of a Christian is to be at worship himself, bringing as many friends as possible to hear the gospel preached. The ultimate absurdity in relation to a home group would be for some to establish a separate group in order to pray for the prayer meeting or to meet separately while the meeting is in progress to pray for those participating! The leader needs to guard against such a false spirituality. It is based on effort rather than trust in God who hears and answers the prayers of those who meet together in his name. It is effectively a religion of works, that seeks to set up an élite group within the fellowship, claiming special favour with God. The leader's task is to encourage the togetherness and unity of the group and to dispel attitudes of spiritual superiority.

He or she is also the one to set prayer targets and to lead the group forward in believing prayer. Group members will have different models from their experience of groups during their college days or from other churches. The leader needs to learn from the suggestions and expectations of his group members, but should give clear guidance about the aim and intent of the praying home group within the context of the wider church. If he is in any doubt about this he should consult with the eldership group.

Shared teaching

The other vital element in the group's programme is Bible study. Many people expect a home group to be primarily a Bible study group, but the St John's concept of 'Open to God' groups means that, in our case, this is not so. The leader must take special care to ensure that the evening is not *dominated* by Bible study. The other elements of praise, worship, intercession, ministry and fellowship must be given adequate time.

If leadership of the Bible study time is shared by different members of the group it is important to draw up a rota of those who are gifted in leading a study and give adequate warning to those required to lead. At some times all the home groups will follow an agreed course of study. At other times the choice will be left to each home group to choose its own course of study. It should be remembered that in the main teaching programme of the church there is a balance between Old Testament and New Testament study and it would be unwise to embark on a study of the Gospels if one of the main teaching series on Sundays is also Gospel-based. It is the leader's responsibility to make sure that the interest of the group is sustained and that there is variety in the Bible study in the course of a year.

Appropriate commentaries and guides to the Bible can be recommended to those who lead the studies. These are to be studied for background information; the information gained from them should not be read out, word for word, at the meeting. But the Bible study leader should be in a position to answer questions that come up regarding doctrines, cross-references and the context of the passage being studied. The art of leadership is to stimulate sharing of biblical insights among the members of the group – not to give heavy, didactic exposition. The leader should help those responsible for the Bible study time to draw out quiet members of the group and to shut up those who are too loquacious. There are very simple means for achieving this – carefully phrased questions, eyes averted so that the over-talkative person cannot intervene too frequently, etc.

Too many shared Bible studies are characterised by Christians sharing their ignorance. The leader of the study should have a sufficient grasp of any complex doctrines covered by the passage, so that mistaken views can be corrected. It is ideal for the home group leader also to have done some background preparation so that more than one member of the group is adequately informed; it is particularly harmful for new Christians to be present when there is disagreement over the meaning of the scriptures. If the Bible study leader has done insufficient homework, matters of dispute could be left over until the next meeting. In the meantime, commentaries should be consulted or the clergy questioned over the points of disagreement. It is better to admit ignorance and offer to find out reasonable answers, than to pontificate in areas of uncertainty.

It is vital to keep the study alive and pertinent. If interest flags, it is better to bring the study to a close and move to another section of the meeting, rather than struggle to keep discussion going. In doing this, the leader should make sure that group members with questions that haven't been answered should feel free to ask questions privately at a later stage of the meeting.

Some might be asked to lead a study who prove to have no gift in doing so. It is important that the leader makes sure everyone in the group understands that gifts of ministry vary from person to person and that although the leadership of Bible studies is likely to be shared around, not everyone will prove to have a notable teaching gift. Thus, not all group members will necessarily lead Bible study. It is unfortunate that often the least gifted people seek leadership and the most gifted wait humbly to be asked to lead. The home group leader must constantly assess the varied abilities of his group members and use them accordingly. For example, if one or two are gifted at leading the worship time, it might be unreasonable to ask them to lead the Bible study as well. The leader's task is to have oversight of the contribution of varied gifts within the group.

Many groups become stuck in a rigid pattern of Bible study. The leader should make it his task to become acquainted with some of the handbooks that are available to give guidance for group Bible study. The aim is not to substitute human inventiveness and imaginativeness for the inspiration of the Holy Spirit, but there is equally no virtue in Bible studies being repetitive and unimaginative.

Boredom is best avoided by presenting expository Bible studies to the group. It is not necessary for the exposition to be high-powered and perfectly prepared, but it has to enable the Bible passage to speak, as the Holy Spirit takes home its meaning, to every member of the group. When the Bible passage is part of an extended plan of sequential Bible study, the purpose for meeting together is clear to everyone. The informal fellowship of the small group becomes a Bible school for learning the deep truths of God. It provides a place for growth in the knowledge of the Lord and for deepening faith, since 'faith comes from hearing the message, and the message is heard through the word of Christ' (Romans 10:17).

Alternative methods of study

While it is important to keep a slot in the programme for specific Bible study (bearing in mind 'the natural man's' desire to choose any other occupation than to get down to serious study of God's word), it is also helpful to use a Christian book as the basis for a course of study over a period of some weeks. This is a particularly good way of helping a group to move in the Spirit. Just as a Lent book can provide invaluable devotional help, so a book on spiritual gifts can lead a group forward both in experience and expectation. In the very early days of charismatic renewal I took a group of young people through the opening chapters of *The Normal Christian Life* by Watchman Nee (Victory Press, 1971). His identification of current twentieth-century manifestations of the Spirit and his relating of these to the happenings of Pentecost enabled us to perceive what God was doing in our midst.

Nee's recurring phrase, 'This is that', helped us to understand that the beginning of our new experience of God was authentically biblical and not just a figment of our imagination. We were at that time a long way off claiming the varied gifts of the Spirit outlined in 1 Corinthians 12, but the gift of teaching (Ephesians 4:11) was most certainly expressed as one of our young people began to expound Paul's letter to the Romans. The rest of us sat open-mouthed as deep, spiritual teaching flowed from his tongue. To do the same thing I would have needed commentaries scattered around my desk, and hours of preparatory study. This sixteen-year-old only opened his mouth and let the teaching flow. At the time we hardly recognised it as a spiritual gift, since we were looking for more spectacular manifestations of the Spirit. On a much later occasion as we were learning how to exercise spiritual gifts at St John's, one of our young schoolteachers made occasional contributions in the mid-week prayer meeting. Whenever she spoke, she seemed to say the final word on the subject under discussion. What is more, her utterances were always given in beautiful and succinct phrases. This was not noticeably her manner of speech in everyday life, and we soon came to recognise that the Holy Spirit was giving her remarkable words of wisdom and mature spirituality.

The group leader has a key job in recognising when such gifts begin to flower. When they are genuinely expressed the person through whom they are given is often diffident and insecure about using their gift, and needs encouragement and help in doing so. In many cases the gifted Christian is quite unaware that God is using them in the group in a notable way. Just as attention-seeking persons can push themselves forward as claimants of spiritual gifts, so the humble group member will hesitate to claim special knowledge or power from God. Wise leadership will recognise the gift and make sure it is expressed for the benefit of the whole group.

Informal fellowship

Any home group is free to meet at any time other than its regular, designated sessions. However, leaders are asked to be mindful of any overall policy for church meetings. If meetings are kept to the minimum, the togetherness of family life is encouraged. If parents are always out at church meetings during weekday evenings and weekends, children often feel neglected and become resentful against the church and Christian activities. In a generation which suffers overmuch from absentee parents, it is an important part of the witness of the church to promote family life and create a sense of security in the lives of children from church families. Single members of home groups may have the opposite problem. They may need extra gatherings in order to develop friendships and to experience the support of church family life. Good leadership will hold these tensions in mind.

Home group Sunday lunches are popular, since children can attend with their parents. Walks can be arranged with shorter distances for the elderly and for those with small children. Children can also be involved in visits to a Christmas play or pantomime, so that the home group fellowship comes to represent a fun time for the whole family.

Obviously the leader must keep in touch with the church diary so that home group events do not clash with family days organised centrally, or with regular annual events like the Harvest Supper or the Parish Weekend.

Some home groups have found it worth while to organise a weekend away for themselves, possibly inviting another group as well. Such weekends should be arranged in consultation with Community Group leaders, church elders and staff, as well as with the church diary. In planning such ventures, the financial implications should also be considered. For example, the strain on family finances could be considerable if a home group weekend away was planned within a three month period either side of a Parish Weekend.

Another way of promoting fellowship is to encourage home group members to invite people from other groups for informal supper parties. If members of the staff team are invited from time to time they will also be helped to get to know members of the congregation at a deeper level. The invitations need to be given personally; they will seldom be taken up as a result of giving out an announcement. It might be good to take up part of a home group evening in arranging a programme of supper parties. Those who are not in a position to offer hospitality should not be threatened by the way it is handled, or be given any sense of being left out. Indeed, such people might be in a position to help another group member who has the facilities for hospitality, but not the time to prepare the food. Good leadership will ensure that all are involved in the hospitality venture, and none feels left out.

Friendships can also be promoted by rotas for some of the 'chore' jobs of church life. If these are tackled on a rota basis, most tasks only come up once a month or so. Jobs might vary from cleaning the worship area, to folding or putting out the service sheets, giving lifts to the blind and handicapped, or helping at the 'Mothers and Toddlers' club. All of these duties provide opportunities to meet other church members in small groups related to the task in hand. In addition to these regular groups organised for practical tasks, others can be formed in order to visit those who are housebound or bereaved. The home group leader could either involve the whole of the home group or those members with sufficient spare time to offer occasional, but regular help.

Giving encouragement

In 1 Thessalonians 2:1–12 Paul describes the integrity of his own ministry among the Christians in Thessalonica. It involved fearless communication of the gospel (v 2): 'with the help of our God we dared to tell you his gospel in spite of strong opposition'. His motives were totally sincere: 'the appeal we make does not spring from error or impure motives, nor are we trying to trick you' (v 3). His ministry was not exercised for any selfish reason, least of all to impress other people: 'We are not trying to please men but God, who tests our hearts . . . We were not looking for praise from men' (vs 4, 6).

The picture he uses to describe his ministry is that of the nursing mother: 'We were gentle among you, like a mother caring for her children' (v 7). It was a ministry of love (v 8). Paul gave of his own being, in order to feed and sustain the young Christians in his care. That is exactly the ministry of the leader of a small group in the church. It calls for self-sacrifice and the exercise of personal discipline, in order to feed others and help them to grow in Christ.

But more than that. Paul also exercises the discipline of a father over the children given into his spiritual care. 'You know that we dealt with each of you as a father deals with his own children, encouraging, comforting and urging you to live lives worthy of God, who calls you into his kingdom and glory' (vs 11–12). Within the discipline of the local church, the small group leader must be in a position to correct wrong attitudes and to encourage godly ways of living with each other in the group. In the wider church the ordained minister has this role and, in a biblically ordered fellowship, it is recognised and accepted. Of course, in ordinary families there are good fathers and bad fathers. Some express the love and control of the heavenly Father in a mature and consistent way. Others have no idea of the heavenly Father's love, and behave utterly selfishly in their human expression of fatherhood, ignoring the needs of their children and failing to reveal to them the true character of the heavenly Father's love and care. In the wider church and in the human family the role of fatherhood is much more clear than in a small group in the church, where the leader may have been singled out in a fairly arbitrary manner. Not everyone in the group is necessarily happy in the choice of their particular leader – indeed some may be secretly resentful of the fact that they were not chosen themselves. However, as the home group leader operates within the overall leadership of the elders, he or she must be in a position to give the firm encouragement of which Paul speaks.

At this point some will ask how a woman can express 'fatherly' care. In the same way, no doubt, that Paul ministered like a 'mother'. Many women are used to exercising an oversight role in their secular duties, whether it is in the classroom, the lecture hall or the office. That does not necessarily mean that they are qualified for spiritual leadership, any more than all men are. Some fellowships base their practice on Paul's teaching that 'the head of every man is Christ, and the head of the woman is man, and the head of Christ is God' (1 Corinthians 11:3), and they forbid all women to exercise such spiritual leadership. Others emphasise the thought, spelt out in the same passage, that 'In the Lord, however, woman is not independent of man, nor is man independent of woman. For as woman came from man, so also man is born of woman. But everything comes from God' (vs 11–12). Each has a different purpose and ability within God's order, but neither can live fully without the other. Many note the liberation that Jesus brought to the place of women in society, and the ministry of women that is recorded in the New Testament as prophetesses (eg the daughters of Philip in Acts) and as servants and workers in the church. Priscilla, for example, was described by Paul as a 'fellow worker in Christ Jesus' (Romans 16:3) and Mary, Tryphena, Tryphosa and Persis, as women who 'work hard in the Lord' (Romans 16:6, 12). In the light of these and other scriptures, there are Christian fellowships where the contribution of women is encouraged, not least in small groups in the church.

This is not the place to debate the issue in full, since there are scholarly works which argue the place in ministry of women in the church. Nonetheless, the issue must be faced in every local church, now that so much spiritual ministry is exercised in the context of small groups and in many places there may be a woman pastor whose ministry is recognised in the wider church.

The essential requirement is that regardless of gender, the authority and leadership of the appointed person is accepted by the group and is supported by the eldership. Then the teaching and care for the group can be expressed with the gentleness of a nursing mother and the strength of a loving father, and the group will learn 'to live lives worthy of God' (1 Thessalonians 2:12).

6
Problems?

If small groups within churches are not formed as part of the strategic growth and outreach of the church, they will form in any case! Such is human need. When groups form in an unplanned and unco-ordinated way, they often represent a spastic or cancerous development in the body of Christ – something uncontrolled and unhelpful, spelling disorder or even death.

There is a strange double-think in the church today. Many argue that small groups – home groups, cells, call them what you will – are essential for achieving the full potential of church life. They provide opportunities for friendship and care, as well as teaching and prayer. And yet if you ask any minister where the problems in his church lie, he will often point at the home groups. 'I cannot get new groups to form,' complains one clergyman. 'They remain introverted fellowships of Christians, and they will not divide when they become too large, or truly welcome new people who want to join.' Another vicar said to me, 'Some of our groups have become holy ghettoes. The members are not only separate from the world, but detached from the church's life as well.' Others complain of a weakness of leadership, with hurried preparation of Bible studies and unimaginative guidance for times of prayer, with an inability to fix goals and attain targets of growth, numerically and in terms of spiritual depth.

Of course, there is another side to the story. Some lay people have to cope with paranoic clergy and ministers who feel threatened when the people they feel called to pastor become spiritual leaders themselves within the home group system. The shepherds find that the sheep have ambitions to fulfil the shepherd's role, or at the very least to bark at the flock and control them like a sheep dog, and that is uncomfortable! The sheep find that they are restrained and confined by overbearing officiousness and authoritarianism, and that is unacceptable. Within the leadership of the church we often do not find shared ministry and mutual goodwill, but misunderstanding, resentment and sometimes annoyed frustration.

Problems! And yet ministers and people, in their better moments, only want to serve the Lord, obey his commands and bring in his kingdom. None really want argument and wrangling within the life of the church. Most clergy and small group leaders simply want to get on with the job. In his narrative poem 'The Minister', R S Thomas describes how the deacons in a Welsh chapel 'chose their pastors as they chose their horses – for hard work . . .' So why don't the ministers get on with it?

The answer is that in so many respects even the highest expressions of ministry in church life have self-interest at their centre. I was at a conference of the Central Stipends Authority of the Church of England in London where we were discussing the pressures and strains on those in the ministry. There was a division of view, in the course of discussion, between those who wanted to keep stipend increases to the minimum in order to identify with those stuck in the poverty trap and those who wanted a definite improvement in the financial circumstances of the clergy in order to enable them to be resource persons in their ministry, unfettered by money worries. I found myself torn in the debate. Both viewpoints could be an expression of responsible love and care, but both could be expressions of self-interest too. The Sir Galahad image of the crusading clergyman, rescuing the poor and the disadvantaged, can easily represent a selfish stance. Identification with the downtrodden can be as insincere as Uriah Heep's claim to be 'very 'umble'. Equally, the desire for monetary reward, with the power and status it gives, can be an obvious path of pursuing self-interest at the expense of giving loving service. But for me the pointed question about ministry came in an informal discussion with a leading diocesan official over lunch. 'Why is it,' he asked, 'that whenever some new venture of ministry is established in a church, it is never the quiet, humble person, who sits with due reticence near the back of church, who offers for the job of leadership, but always the busy, pushing person, who is already a leading light on the Church Council and sits on half a dozen church committees as well?' My rather cynical answer was to suggest that because of the degree of self-interest in so much of the work we do (allegedly for God) in the life of the church, it is probably because such a person needs a platform for self expression. So many tasks are taken on because of the kudos they provide. Often, a person who is frustrated by a lack of promotion at work, or a lack of fulfilment in home and family turns to opportunities of 'ministry' in the church to find personal well-being and satisfaction. It is a very human and understandable thing to do, but inevitably such self-interest mars ministry. When it is the motivation for leadership of a home group, problems are bound to arise.

Divisiveness

Self-interest also ruins the life of a group when members rise up in protest against their leaders. I have known situations where certain members of a small home group have formed a clique of criticism against the leaders of the group. Others have sensed the feeling of hostility and the uncomfortable atmosphere of criticism and resentment, and have closed ranks with the leaders in order to give them encouragement and support. Instead of creating unity, this act of solidarity has only deepened division.

To the extent that this is Satan's work, as he is always the author of division in the church and uses every weakness of Christians to pull the church apart, the fundamental reason for the disagreement is usually both trivial and predictable. Christians who express their shared faith in the unity of the godhead, as they say the creed Sunday by Sunday, easily fall out over forms of baptism, issues of predestination and free will, and in these days the whole question of renewal by the Holy Spirit and its expression. Some want free worship with jolly choruses, other want times of silence and reflection. Some hope for the regular expression of the gifts of the Spirit, others feel threatened when the gifts are used.

At St John's, Harborne, we have a phrase to describe our praise and prayer times and also our small groups. We use it in order to avoid the sort of division and controversy described above. We ask that every Christian should be 'open to God'. The keen charismatic person will then be sensitive and open to what God is saying about the use of spiritual gifts at a particular time and in a particular group. He might long for a greater freedom in worship and in sharing what life in the Spirit is all about, but he will not insist that all the gifts are used all the time if it is not yet right or possible for the group to operate that way.

Abuse of community

Some expressions of self-interest are more subtle. Because so many people today have lost a sense of community, and live lonely lives as isolated units of humanity, the small group in a church can be used as a substitute family. That, of course, may be part of its *raison d'être* within the structure of a church. However, a selfish child or parent in a natural family unit, who sets out to 'get' rather than to 'give' soon finds that he or she is contributing to the breakdown of family life rather than to its proper growth and development. This need for fulfilment through participation in community life is seen in the tremendous fascination for TV soap operas. One headmaster became so hooked on 'Neighbours', soon after it began to be shown in Britain, that he recommended all his staff watch it. He put up a notice on his office door – 'Meeting in Progress' – in order to be free to watch it undisturbed, claiming that it was essential for every headmaster to know what his pupils were looking at!

The point this man was making is that at the heart of all soaps we find a community. By following the soaps, lost and lonely people can have community interests and community involvement, even if in a fictional, second-hand way. It is not surprising, therefore, if people use fictional communities in this way that some also use *real* communities to satisfy their own inner needs, rather than finding them to be spheres in which they can love and serve other people. Such attitudes are to be expected because of normal human selfishness, but it does nonetheless present a serious problem for the life of a small group, if one or more of the members regularly *use* it to live out their own fantasies and needs.

This abuse of community can take many forms. Sometimes it is seen in the response of a group member to leadership and authority figures. In the wider church congregation there will always be those with hang-ups about the vicar or pastor, because he is seen as the strong, dominating leader who thunders the stern word of God from a church pulpit which is designed to be a full six feet above anyone's contradiction. The expression of authority is further emphasised by priestly or academic robes or even the crisply styled suiting of those whose tradition does not embrace distinctive robes for the minister. He nonetheless manages to make himself noticeably authoritative by other means. I was once amused to be greeted by a student at the back of our church, who saw me close up for the very first time, and said, 'Oh! You don't look nearly so frightening at close quarters!' The rather grand and bright Birmingham Canon's robes had created quite a false impression of grandeur at a distance, that had perhaps got mixed up with his own inner difficulties in coping with any authority figure.

Authoritarianism

The imputation of authority or, more usually, authoritarianism can create problems within a small group too. When a group member cringes before the leader of a sub-group in the church, tensions and difficulties can spread to everyone else within the tight-knit community. Whether the relationship hang-up is expressed by a sullen silence or by querulous criticism, the unhappiness spreads rapidly. The self-interest of the disgruntled person destroys any possibility of growing in prayer and deep

Bible study, since the bad feeling grieves the Spirit of God as well as harming human relationships. A primary purpose of small groups in the life of a church is to enable Christian people to learn to live together in harmonious relationships and thus to overcome the self-interest which destroys community. It is truly perverse that the group which is formed to serve God and to serve others, and which is intended to be a sphere of love and trust, actually provides the opportunity for expressing dominating attitudes and cherishing inner resentments. A fine spiritual director of the late seventeenth and early eighteenth centuries, François de Fenelon, Archbishop of Cambrai, showed in his writings that this is no new problem: 'Almost all who aim at serving God do so more or less for their own sake. They want to win, not to lose; to be comforted, not to suffer; to possess, not to be despoiled; to increase, not to diminish. Yet all the while our whole interior progress consists in losing, sacrificing, decreasing, humbling and stripping self even of God's own gifts, so as to be wholly His.'

Wrong authoritarianism creeps in when the leaders are not willing to lose, sacrifice, and decrease in importance. True love is always giving; the firm but humble leader will always be giving prominence to others, not always claiming it for himself. How can we avoid authoritarianism? Here are some tips for the leader:

- Ensure that tasks of leadership in worship, teaching and prayer are shared around the group.
- Ensure that meetings are not always held on your home premises, where you will have a natural and unfair advantage as host or hostess.
- Be careful that you do not show any favouritism. Human beings naturally form into groupings within which they feel secure for social, educational or professional reasons. Leadership 'feels' authoritarian and heavy-handed if those leading take advantage of their role to be always choosing certain friends for tasks and duties within the group. Favouritism is often shown in society at large, but must be avoided in church life.
- Be determined to share the decision-making process,

regarding courses of study, pattern of meetings, etc, with others in the group. A system of shared leadership works better than one which depends on one person making unilateral decisions. Further, this prevents the group from becoming wrongly dependent on one leader. In addition, others share the load of pastoral care and in turn become equipped to lead their own group.

- Try to be more concerned about the growth and development of the group members than about your own status and importance in the leadership role. By doing this the new 'commandment' of Jesus is fulfilled, as is the exhortation of Romans 15:1: 'We who are strong ought to bear with the failings of the weak and not to please ourselves. Each of us should please his neighbour for his good, to build him up.'

Rivalry and gossip

In a moment of pulpit exaggeration, I once cried out in despair to a congregation which was in danger of destroying itself by constant mutual criticism and backbiting, 'I would rather discover that every member of the Church Council is in a state of adultery than have the very being of the church ruined by seething gossip!' The point I was making was that an obvious and open sin like adultery can be challenged and disciplined. It can be dealt with by confronting the wrong-doers and challenging them with the standard of God's law. The offenders can repent and, when they have shown amendment of life, can be restored to fellowship. But the rivalry engendered by gossip and slanderous talk cannot be measured or controlled so easily. Self-interested and dissatisfied people draw the innocent into their carping criticism, and even those who normally have no desire to engage in the destruction of other people's reputations, find themselves quickly caught up in it.

James warns us in his letter that the tongue can do damage out of all proportion to its size: 'The tongue also is a fire, a world of evil among the parts of the body. It corrupts the whole person, sets the whole course of his life on fire, and is itself set on fire by hell . . . no man can tame the tongue. It is a restless evil, full of deadly poison. With the tongue we praise our Lord and Father, and with it we curse men, who have been made in God's likeness. Out of the same mouth come praise and cursing. My brothers, this should not be' (James 3:6, 8–10). Later he says, 'Don't grumble against each other, brothers, or you will be judged. The Judge is standing at the door' (James 5:9). James is not alone in highlighting the destructive nature of envious, critical and judgmental attitudes that pour out through the tongue. After Paul has listed the evil qualities at the heart of the 'old' self, and contrasted them with the Jesus-like qualities of a Spirit-filled Christian, he urges, 'keep in step with the Spirit. Let us not become conceited, provoking and envying each other' (Galatians 5:25–26).

Insecurity

While such rivalry and criticism cannot be tolerated in a group of Christian people, and the art of leadership is to deal with it in a correcting and loving way, it has to be recognised that such attitudes often stem from a hurt background. The offending person needs care and understanding as well as admonition. Just as strong leadership sometimes cannot be accepted if it is a reminder of heavy-handed parental authority, so the love and warmth expressed by Christians in a small group can challenge painfully the lack of love in a needy person's background. Any counsellor aware of another person's body language will have noticed a damaged person wince physically whenever the word 'love' is mentioned. A lack of love leads to a very low self-image. A child can grow up feeling uncomfortable and unwanted within a loving community. Instead of the Christian group proving to be the place of healing and welcome, it proves in practice to be a place that feels like threat and rejection. It highlights the needy person's inability either to receive loving overtures from others, or to respond with love in return. And yet there is a sense of Christian duty that compels attendance at the home group meetings. The group is small enough for any one member to be missed, and the thought of the leader making a friendly pastoral call later in the week to ask why one was missing, is even worse than the pain of enduring yet another meeting. Some avoid this agony by resolving never ever to join such a group, but others fail to escape the initial pressure from the minister to join a group and continue with a growing sense of resentment and pain.

It is this tension that bursts out in criticism. If a person with a low self image cannot cope with the strength of other people's love, he or she has to knock it down to size. Only then can the hurt person sustain their own membership of the loving group. By making others out to be weak and imperfect, his own strength is enhanced and he can compensate for his feelings of inferiority and weakness. Sometimes, as with a bereaved person, there is an almost compulsive need to damage those who care most of all for you. This explains the virulence of criticism that stems from a broken heart.

Relationships in the small group may also be complicated by the fact that the leader might carry areas of damage from the past. He is not perfect any more than the members of his group are. He may counter criticism with more officious and authoritarian leadership or he may react with personal resentment against his opponent. *He* is then stirred into attitudes of self-interest – defending himself against criticism and possibly stirring up further gossip against the one who is threatening his position in the group. Others soon pick up the unhappy atmosphere even if they are not personally involved on one side or the other.

I remember being trapped in this sort of controversy on one occasion and, in a moment of vulnerability, blurted out the problem to Bishop Hugh Montefiore, soon after he had arrived as our bishop in Birmingham. 'And how are things going with you in the parish?' he asked. I felt like saying that things could not be worse just at that time. We seemed to be divided up into factions. As leader I was heavily under criticism. Where there should have been loving fellowship and unity there was appalling criticism and backbiting. In reacting to the complaints with hard words, I was not exempt from blame. 'Can you conceive it possible,' I asked the bishop, 'that a group of Christian people can destroy each other with bitter and jealous words? I am at my wits' end and just do not know where to turn next. Do I cave in and leave the parish or fight it through?' 'You neither run away nor fight,' he wisely advised. 'You simply accept the situation. You accept that this is what a ministry is all about. You see that this is exactly what Jesus took on the cross, and as *he* bore the sin and suffering of others, so do you.'

Of course, I knew that all the time. Sometimes, however, it needs another person to say the obvious thing, so that we can allow a shaft of light into the mess of tangled relationships that develop when Christian people allow self-interest and sin to predominate in the church's life.

As far as the small group is concerned, the answer to such disorder should be found within the wider structure of the church's life. A pattern of lay eldership or ministerial oversight can provide the sort of intervention that Bishop Hugh did for me. Sometimes however, the structure may be there, but the personalities in conflict may not be willing to receive outside help. It may be, in such an instance, that things have to get worse before they can improve. Sometimes I have found such an *impasse* to have developed that no amount of good advice leads to any improvement at all. The only thing to do is to wait for the healing of friendships within the sovereignty of God's timing. We can pray, but we cannot hurry the gradual process of reconciliation.

Juan Carlos Ortiz concurred with this view when he stayed in our home during a preaching visit to Birmingham. His church in Argentina had known a remarkable moving of God's Spirit, and his writings show considerable insight into problems of discipleship and leadership within the local church. I asked him: 'When the members of our church and our home groups hurt each other by rivalry and gossip, and grieve the Spirit of God by wrong talk and dissension, do we work at disciplining the membership so that – with repentance and renewed faith – we can move forward in the Spirit? Or do we live with the disorder, knowing that God looks with mercy on our human frailty, and will yet move among us in power and love?' Of course, I knew the answer before the question was out of my mouth: 'You will never create a perfect fellowship out of sinful human beings,' he replied. 'Trust God to make you new.'

The answer to problems of disagreement and disorder in the fellowship of the church is to give time for God to work out his good purposes in answer to believing prayer. The temptation for some leaders is to intervene immediately and in a heavy-handed way to correct the wrong. In family life, the art of parenting is often expressed in the timing and in the strength of correction of children. Right parental authority demands good relationships of love and mutual care, but a wrong authoritarianism can lead to further rebellion and greater disarray. The secret of our family togetherness has always been to remind each other, 'We are a Jesus family; we do not behave like that.' Leadership in the church can be similarly expressed, whether it is the leader and his home group or the vicar and his PCC or the wider congregation.

If the temptation for some is to jump in too quickly with heavy rebuke, the mistake of others is to allow disputes to fester over long periods of time. I belonged to one church where two ladies had not spoken to each other for over forty years, and yet they knelt side by side at the communion rail Sunday after Sunday! Such disarray needs reproof. Unfortunately, because the disagreement had not been settled years before, the best time for bringing the two injured parties together had no doubt long since passed, but in my view it was vital for the pastor to tackle the conflict and bring God's healing to it. Paul urges repentance on the part of two quarrelling women in Philippians 4:2: 'I plead with Euodia and I plead with Syntyche to agree with each other in the Lord.' He is open about the problem but urges gentleness in dealing with the women concerned: 'I ask you, loyal yoke-fellow, help these women who have contended at my side in the cause of the gospel' (v 3). In the Pastoral epistles he speaks many times against murmuring, grumbling and quarrelling, as though it was as much a characteristic of groups of Christians in the early church as it is, sadly, in some churches today. Among other things, he writes that a leader must not be 'quarrelsome' (1 Timothy 3:3) and his qualities for leadership must be clearly expressed in his natural family. 'He must manage his own family well and see that his children obey him with proper respect'

(3:4). In 2 Timothy 2:14 Paul exhorts: 'Warn them before God against quarrelling about words; it is of no value and only ruins those who listen.' Again, 'the Lord's servant must not quarrel; instead, he must be kind to everyone, able to teach, not resentful' (2:24).

It is comforting to know that 'human nature being what it is', the Christians of New Testament days found it just as easy as we do to fall out with each other, and to spoil the quality of heavenly fellowship and God-centred worship that should characterise all gatherings of the people of God. Some are deeply disillusioned when they find redeemed sinners behaving like sinners and not like rescued saints. I ask people to be positive, truthful and realistic. The fact that sin and selfishness is expressed in both small and large groups of Christians gathering together within the life of a local church only proves the Bible to be true. 'Yes,' we say, 'the heart is deceitful above all things and beyond cure' (Jeremiah 17:9). This side of the grave we do, constantly have to turn away from sin, and fight Satan at every turn. The Bible reveals that we are spoilt, marred, broken, self-centred creatures, who often love this world and its ways better than the heavenly Kingdom. We profess loudly to love the King, but fail in obedience to him every day.

But God is at work within us by his Spirit. One here and one there is being more and more conformed to the wholeness of Jesus and it is our privilege within our groups to see that happening and to allow it in our own experience too. Thus, within the problems and difficulties, there are glimpses of grace, signs of goodness, experiences of love. We can be full of hope that God will be working to produce evidence of his character and of Kingdom standards within the unpromising soil of groups of humans joined together in Christ and open to the working of God's Spirit. Our call is to take part in all that God is doing, and to help each group member to full maturity in the knowledge of God's word and so in the work of the Kingdom: 'All Scripture is God-breathed and is useful for teaching, rebuking, correcting and training in righteousness, so that the man of God may be thoroughly equipped for every good work' (2 Timothy 3:16–17).

7
Support
for
leaders

Asking for the vision of every-member ministry to be fulfilled puts a big demand on small group leaders. But no one is ever alone in the leadership task. We are always 'God's fellow-workers' (2 Corinthians 6:1). Jesus is not just a leadership example to look back to. We have in him 'a great High Priest over the house of God' (Hebrews 10:21). As the High Priest in Old Testament days directed the priesthood of Israel in its spiritual leadership, so today, as the privileges of priesthood in terms of direct access to God have been passed on to all Christian believers, we can all look to Jesus for his direction of our lives and ministry. Unfortunately, a mistaken view of priesthood in the church that still sees those in the ordained ministry as being specialist, professional intermediaries between the believer and God, has led to an underrating of each individual believer's status and standing in God's service. Lay ministry, which has to predominate in the small group structure, is often seen as amateur and second-rate. A bishop in the church once warned me of the danger of allowing lay people to 'meddle in spiritual ministry'. And yet every-member ministry is exactly what was made possible by Christ's death on the cross. Each of us now has the confidence of direct access to God: 'Therefore, brothers, since we have confidence to enter the Most Holy Place by the blood of Jesus, by a new and living way opened for us through the curtain, that is, his body, and since we have a great priest over the house of God, let us draw near to God with a sincere heart, in full assurance of faith, having our hearts sprinkled to cleanse us from a guilty conscience and having our bodies washed with pure water' (Hebrews 10:19–22).

New Testament Christianity is not about holy mysteries performed in a holy place by holy people. Indeed, we have seen that the early church did not have holy buildings in which to worship. Necessity demanded a home-based spiritual ministry, with the body of believers themselves forming the 'holy temple' through which the life of God is expressed in the world. Paul, writing to believers at Corinth asked, 'Don't you know that you yourselves are God's temple and that God's Spirit lives in you?' (1 Corinthians 3:16.) As the Holy Spirit has been poured out on every believer there is now no specialist priesthood that can hold privileges of ministry to itself. Indeed, men and women of all ages and classes are being given gifts of the Spirit for ministry. 'In the last days', God says, 'I will pour out my Spirit on all people. Your sons and daughters will prophesy, your young men will see visions, your old men will dream dreams. Even on my servants, both men and women, I will pour out my Spirit in those days and they will prophesy.' (Acts 2:17–18, quoting from Joel 2.) As the Spirit was poured out at Pentecost on 'each one' of the disciples, so gifts for leadership and ministry are poured out on each Christian within the body of Christ. 'All these are the work of one and the same Spirit, and he gives them to each one, just as he determines' (1 Corinthians 12:11).

So, with confidence in approaching God and with confidence in his gifts and resources for ministry, we can persevere gladly in the task of mutual ministry within our small groups, expressing the priesthood of all believers. The writer of the letter to the Hebrews applies his exhortation to the practicalities of working out relationships in the church. The wording smacks of the sort of issues that relate specifically to small group ministry: 'Let us consider how we may spur one another on towards love and good deeds. Let us not give up meeting together, as some are in the habit of doing, but let us encourage one another – and all the more as you see the Day approaching' (Hebrews 10:24–25).

There is a corporateness about ministry in the New Testament which demands the existence of small groups for its proper expression. As Paul describes the experience of early church worship in 1 Corinthians 14:26 and following, there was opportunity for everyone to contribute – something manifestly impossible in a worship gathering of several hundred people: 'When you come together, everyone has a hymn, or a word of instruction, a revelation, a tongue or an interpretation . . . if anyone speaks in a tongue, two or at the most three should speak, one at a time, and someone must interpret . . . Two or three prophets should speak, and the others should weigh carefully what is said.' Numbers are clearly small for such controlled expression of mutual ministry, and clear overall direction and leadership is expected.

Peter emphasises this sense of mutual belonging of the Spirit-filled fellowship of believers when he speaks of the church as 'a chosen people, a royal priesthood, a holy nation, a people belonging to God' (1 Peter 2:9). Here the privilege of belonging to Christ and being under his High Priesthood is seen not only in terms of our access to God as priests, but as a sharing of his royal rule. The church is a 'royal priesthood'. We are, through the cross, made to be 'a kingdom of priests to serve his God and Father' (Revelation 1:6). This does not at all mean that as Christians we are called to express a heavy-handed monarchical authority, though there are some branches of the church where leadership takes a very dominating and authoritarian form. Rather, as we meet together we are meant to demonstrate to the world what it means to be a people of the kingdom of God. Leaders will combine both the authority and gentleness of Jesus the King. Members of our groups will show a right acceptance of leadership, a right expression of mutual care and ministry and a right response to God in prayer and worship. The love, acceptance, respect and obedience shown both to God and to fellow Christians should display the outworking of the kingdom on earth. As we meet as 'kings and priests' we should demonstrate in our relationships the answer to our Lord's prayer, 'your kingdom come, your will be done on earth as it is in heaven' (Matthew 6:10).

Shared eldership

Leaders must be willing to be led – ultimately of course by the Holy Spirit of God. If there is opportunity in a church's structure for every-member ministry to be expressed, for instance, through home group leaders and members, there needs to be a shared eldership in the church to avoid the wrong sort of authoritarianism in the leading of leaders. There must be a leadership within which there is sufficient mutual trust and respect for one to be corrected by another or, if necessary, by the group of leaders together. As we have seen, Paul committed the charge of a newly established church to a group of elders. While Paul was at Antioch the church was given warning of a great famine, through the prophet Agabus; and Paul and Barnabas were sent to Jerusalem, to the elders, with a gift from the Christians at Antioch. Later, the same partnership was sent out by the church at Antioch to preach the gospel and plant churches throughout the region. On the way back to Antioch, 'Paul and Barnabas appointed elders for them in each church and, with prayer and fasting, committed them to the Lord in whom they had put their trust' (Acts 14:23). Again in Antioch, there was controversy in the church when some teachers came down from Judea insisting that Christians should conform to the demands of the Jewish law. In particular they insisted, 'Unless you are circumcised, according to the custom taught by Moses, you cannot be saved' (15:1). Following sharp dispute and argument with them, Paul and Barnabas were again sent out by the church 'to go up to Jerusalem to see the apostles and elders about this question' (15:2).

This pattern of shared eldership is fundamental to the organisation of the early church. It is in complete contrast to the concept of 'one man ministry' that characterises most churches today. Many have no existing structure for accommodating such shared leadership. Some have experimented with various schemes of lay eldership in which pastoral oversight is shared with those who are ordained, but it has to be confessed that not all the experiments have been successful.

At St John's, Harborne, we established an eldership in what we thought to be an open, democratic and also a truly spiritual way. As vicar I did not appoint elders according to Paul's apostolic pattern, since I was to be one of the elders myself. We drew together a group of some two dozen people to pray and study the Scriptures weekly, until we could be sure of God's way ahead for us. This group was in addition to the 'Open to God' praise meeting and the smaller home groups, and met over a period of twelve months. It comprised seven full-time paid staff, six lay readers, six members of the standing committee plus other leaders from the church council, parish organisations and from the congregation itself. Invitations were given to all these groups, and very few offered to join the venture apart from those already deeply committed in leadership. When it came to asking if any of the congregation felt called to take part, we stipulated that those who offered should be interviewed by the existing leadership and then accepted, or rejected if considered unsuitable. In the event only three volunteered, of whom two were accepted and one was turned down.

By the end of our studies we were convinced about the importance of plurality in eldership, but also that one person had to be *primus inter pares*. Inevitably, in a typical anglican parish, that person was the vicar. In order to find out who the elders should be from among our wider group, we asked that any person who had a sense of call from God to eldership, should indicate that this was the case. We also asked everyone in the group to nominate those whom they felt were called to the task. Just three of the laymen's names were on both lists, and we concluded that these should join the three who had already been ordained as presbyters in the church, to form a shared eldership. This plan was approved by the Church Council, which still retained its official decision-making role, especially in matters involving the expenditure of money. The one proviso that the Church Council made was that if anything should go wrong in the functioning of the eldership, the vicar and the Church Council should resume their shared role of oversight as before. Furthermore, it was agreed that elders should always be drawn from the ranks of the Church Council, which meant that they had to be voted into office each year at the church's Annual General Meeting. Only very recently, after some fifteen years, has this latter requirement been relaxed.

The proposals were then taken to the Parochial Annual General Meeting and approved by the church. The experiment was also noted by the bishop. After some initial difficulties during which the harmony of the eldership group was severely tested, other senior laymen were added to the eldership and for many years the leadership of the elders in spiritual matters has been greatly valued by the church.

Smoothing the way

Over those years a number of snags have emerged, and the lessons learnt from these apply to the running of any small group in the church.

Firm leadership

Firstly, in my desire as vicar not to dominate the group, I failed to give firm enough leadership. This encouraged others among the eldership who were strong leaders in their own right, especially those in secular spheres of work, to press their own vision. At times some felt understandably disappointed if their firm and well-thought-out opinion did not prevail. Although it is perfectly obvious to us now that each of six firmly-held ideas cannot all be right and cannot all find expression at any one time, we did not find it easy at first to surrender our views to one another and to yield on our particular issue when it was necessary. Equally, it could not be right that we achieved agreement only at the level of the lowest common denominator, the church going forward on the basis of compromise decisions. It was at this point that my own leadership was weakest, for I would often infuriate others in the group by seeming to agree on a matter one week and then, after thinking and praying the matter through, I would ask for the decision to be reversed the following week. This would be due to the fact that I might possess extremely confidential information about a person or a subject under discussion, which

I did not feel free to share even with that senior group. In the event, the others had to choose either to trust my judgment or to be annoyed with me for putting a spanner into the works! If I had been stronger in leadership at an earlier stage in the deliberations I might have avoided a lot of heartache. Equally of course, I might have been legitimately accused of being too strong and dominating and thus I might have hindered free sharing and discussion.

Part of our problem was that all of us wanted to be decision-making executives, whereas spiritual ministry is not just about making decisions and exercising a power of eldership. We should have known from our earlier 'Open to God' sessions that the main priority in church life is to put *God's* will into action. Instead of taking time to discover God's will, we now listed all the areas of church life where decisions needed to be made, and we sought to put *our* programme into effect.

Defining areas of responsibility

It was when we turned to practical action that the value of the shared eldership was discovered. From time to time, as need arose in the church, we held an elders' healing service. People in need of prayer were brought by their friends or counsellors and, in the context of a quiet communion service, the elders would pray for individuals who came forward and anoint them with oil. It was not that we claimed special powers of healing, but took seriously the injunction of James 5:14: 'Is any one of you sick? He should call the elders of the church to pray over him and anoint him with oil in the name of the Lord.' Further, we saw that 'the prayer offered in faith will make the sick person well' (v 15). We therefore saw that our qualification for this ministry lay not in possessing special gifts of healing given by the Holy Spirit, but in our obedience and believing prayer. *We* took responsibility for prayer, which is so often difficult for a sick person, and exercised *our* faith in a God who heals.

The sense of God's power released in dramatic healings restored our confidence in the rightness of God's call to us as elders. The problem was in the dynamics of our small eldership group. We needed to accept each other afresh with forgiveness and love. When this was done we looked for further ways to express eldership in a more outgoing style of practical ministry.

Here we made another mistake. In order to ensure that each elder had a specific area of responsibility, we gave each one a number of small home groups to pastor. The elders were asked to meet with the leaders and deputy leaders of a number of groups, because we had a corporate vision to be advisers for them on particular aspects of need or difficulty. But we found that not all the elders had the right sort of pastoral gift for doing this job satisfactorily. Some, by their manner of dealing with the small group leaders, *created* problems rather than solved them!

We found that our ministry as elders was most effective when we *divided* our energies among the various tasks that needed oversight in the life of the church. All of us then separated according to our various gifts and strengths. Not all were asked to be pastors, counsellors or experts in administration, but each one operated according to his ability. Some specialised in caring for the home group leaders, while others concentrated on running a programme of training for those involved in the church's counselling ministry. Some advised on church fabric and buildings, while others gave vocational advice and introduced a scheme called 'Living Stones' which provided better financial support for those going forward into full-time Christian work. Some gave themselves to guide our evangelistic ventures, while others advised on all aspects related to worship. At last we had found a pattern of eldership that worked – so much so that others with the qualities and abilities of eldership could be drawn into the small eldership groups, working on these various aspects of the life and ministry of the church, without each one having to be formally appointed as an elder.

The pattern of working became free and flexible, with each elder knowing his or her responsibility for a certain area of church life. We no longer had the bottleneck of an eldership which together had to consider almost every aspect of the church's life and mission before anything could be done. Furthermore, while this system works effectively we are not trapped into a 'hierarchy' system where we have to create more and more elders as more people rise to a seniority of ministry in the church. Indeed, the emphasis has been on elders being willing to stand down, either because of age, busyness or deteriorating health. Certainly all will stand down when a new vicar is appointed so that, as a new man begins his ministry, he will be free to form his own team under God and establish a new group for the next period of leadership in the church.

Mutual trust and support

The need to take this step was brought home to me while ministering in another church, where a new vicar had inherited a splendid and strong team of elders from his predecessor. Unfortunately they just could not let go. They had always been used to making decisions about the affairs of the church and they were overruled to the point where he felt he could not exercise his *own* particular gifts of ministry. He did not wish to appear obstructive and wished at all costs to avoid direct conflict with such competent colleagues. But he simply could not work within the demands that they put on him and became down-hearted and discouraged.

In the small group of leaders that is represented by such an eldership team, total trust and mutual acceptance are essential. If the team leader has *invited* others to be his co-workers or if, as in St John's case, a number of people had spent months of heartfelt prayer together, working to discover those God was calling to the task, there is a basic obligation to make the group work. This is how it is with any small group where the members feel truly committed in love to one another. In the case of an eldership team there is the added bonus of the sense of privilege in being called to such a position of trust, respect and seniority of leadership. If the elders remain as a hangover from a previous regime, these conditions do not prevail to the same degree. Dynamically it is easier for the existing lay elders to gang up together against the new pastor, with whom at first there is hardly likely to be a deep relationship of trust. This is why it is very much wiser for the elders to stand down *en bloc*, indicating their availability for service if the new pastor is disposed to use them.

Coping with personality clashes

A further factor in the dynamics of such a group is the question of personality clash. Hopefully this may be a rare occurrence within a Christian community, but it does happen. The deeper the love relationships go in a church, the easier it is to find that we *can* love some brothers and sisters in Christ, although in terms of attitude and personality we do not get on at all. We might not even 'like' the other person at a natural level. No pious view that personality clashes should not happen in the church overcomes this natural human aversion. It is part of the Fall and part of the self-centredness of our lives. God is undoubtedly working on our weaknesses by his Spirit, and we are no doubt claiming his grace for our human frailty. But the fact remains that there are some people whom we can love in the Lord whom we can find exceedingly difficult to work with. The reason for this is that, at an *ordinary* level of human and indeed Christian involvement, it is possible to steer away from issues of controversy and difference. Indeed, within a small fellowship group it is possible for wide-ranging views to be expressed in a learning situation without those who hold contrasting points of view becoming bitterly divided. At an eldership level it is different. Every matter on an agenda can be potentially contentious. If there is a personality clash to deal with on top of disagreements that have to be expressed within the normal course of discussion, with an already full agenda, there is a recipe for trouble.

Such a clash occurred even within the enthusiasm of the early church's evangelistic programme. The clash was between Paul and John Mark. The latter had previously let Paul down, so when Barnabas suggested taking him with them on a tour of the churches, 'Paul did not think it wise to take him, because he had deserted them in Pamphylia and had not continued with them in the work' (Acts 15:38). Such behaviour was so contrary to Paul's style of perseverance and total self-sacrifice in God's work, that it is indeed hard to see how the pair of them could easily work together at close quarters again. Sadly, this clash between Paul and John Mark led to a serious conflict and argument between Paul and Barnabas. By this time they had become close companions, having travelled far in each other's company, preaching the gospel and building up the churches. Clearly there is no evidence of a previous personality clash between these two. If Paul was an aggressive, purposeful person, Barnabas was, as his name suggested, a true 'son of encouragement'. He seemed to be the easiest person in the world to get on with. When he saw 'the evidence of the grace of God, he was glad and encouraged them to remain true to the Lord with all their hearts. He was a good man, full of the Holy Spirit and faith' (Acts 11:23–24). The sad effect of Paul's clash with John Mark was that his partnership with Barnabas was broken. He and Barnabas 'had such a sharp disagreement that they parted company' (Acts 15:39).

This is the practical answer to serious dispute – to agree not to work together for a while. Their fundamental love for each other in the Lord is not denied, but their ability to work together in leadership is temporarily lost. Often this sort of genuine disagreement, where two sincere people see the same issue from totally conflicting viewpoints, is only resolved over a period of time. Each must, of course, seek to relate to the other with an attitude of repentance and forgiveness, until eventually the wound and the dispute is completely healed. Interestingly, the original personality clash between Paul and John Mark which led to the break-up of the partnership between Paul and Barnabas, was also eventually put right. As an old man, Paul asked Timothy in the last letter he wrote, 'Get Mark and bring him with you, because he is helpful to me in my ministry' (2 Timothy 4:11).

If the possibility of dispute is constantly present amongst the most senior leadership of Spirit-filled Christians, it is potentially possible at any level of relationship in the church. Elders do well to take special care, if that is their calling, of the leaders of small groups, committed to their charge. If the close working friendship of two men like Barnabas and Paul can be threatened by the defection of a young man who had previously toured with them (see Acts 12:25), then every leader needs to work hard at maintaining strong bonds of friendship and love, even where there are personality differences. But we are also all engaged in spiritual warfare, and this will bring suffering in its wake.

Prepared for suffering

When Paul spoke to the Ephesian elders he warned of conflict that could be stirred up in the church fellowship through human perverseness and hostility, both from outside and inside the church. When Peter gave specific instructions to elders he warned of the conflict in terms of direct spiritual attack from Satan, the enemy of souls. His teaching was in the context of a warning about the trials and suffering his hearers could expect to endure: 'Dear friends, do not be surprised at the painful trial you are suffering, as though something strange were happening to you. But rejoice that you participate in the sufferings of Christ, so that you may be overjoyed when his glory is revealed' (1 Peter 4:12–13).

When Jesus spoke of glory, he referred to that quality which he shared with the Father in heaven before he came to earth, but he was also meaning his obedience in accepting the suffering of death on the cross. He prayed to the Father, 'Father, the time has come. Glorify your Son that your Son may glorify you . . . I have brought you glory on earth by completing the work you gave me to do. And now, Father, glorify me in your presence with the glory I had with you before the world began' (John 17:1, 4–5).

The same theme of glory runs through Peter's address to the elders of the church. The sharing in Christ's sufferings is 'so that you may be overjoyed when his glory is revealed' (1 Peter 4:13). Peter speaks of himself as 'one who also will share in the glory to be revealed' (5:1). Those who are eager to serve in eldership, as true examples to the flock, 'will receive the crown of glory that will never fade away' (v 4). And if this is in one sense a *reward* for service, it is also a *gift* that goes with God's call, for, 'the God of all grace, who called you to his eternal glory in Christ, after you have suffered a little while, will himself restore you and make you strong, firm and steadfast' (v 10).

We are heading for 'eternal glory,' which is what Jesus enjoyed with the Father before he came to earth. Everything that he enjoyed he gives to us, and although our ministry to others may lead us into a degree of hardship and suffering, the compensation is in what we receive from God through Christ. He brings eternal reality and glory into our earthly circumstances. Just before his death, Paul wrote to Timothy urging him not to 'be ashamed to testify about our Lord' (2 Timothy 1:8). If he was to be a leader in the church, knowing the power of God, salvation from sins, and the call 'to a holy life' (v 9), Timothy had to be willing to share in suffering too. The 'eternal glory' for which we are heading in Christ is made real to us in the rough and tumble of daily Christian life and ministry.

The gifts of God in Christ are power, forgiveness, holiness and resurrection life, and our ministry in the church needs to be exercised at this level of spiritual reality. Again, these qualities of Christian life are not to be experienced only by ordained ministers, even though Paul is writing to Timothy, reminding him to 'fan into flame the gift of God, which is in you through the laying on of . . . hands' (2 Timothy 1:6). Much earlier in his life, when he was writing to Christians in the church at Corinth, Paul also spoke of ministry in the context of glory and eternity: 'Since through God's mercy we have this ministry, we do not lose heart' (2 Corinthians 4:1). From the context we see that 'this ministry' is Christ's ministry – the ministry of the gospel, of the Spirit, and of the new covenant. Paul contrasts the ministry of the new covenant with that of the old. 'We are not like Moses,' he writes (2 Corinthians 3:13). After he had met with God he had to put a veil over his face to prevent the Israelites seeing the radiance which had 'rubbed off' on him. But we can not only reflect the Lord's glory, we 'are being transformed into his likeness with ever-increasing glory, which comes from the Lord, who is the Spirit' (2 Corinthians 3:18). As another translation puts it, we are 'being changed into his likeness from one degree of glory to another' (RSV).

Glory and ministry go together, and this is as true for the small group leader in a church as it is for the full-time ordained minister. To engage in pastoral care is to take on the burdens of others. The suffering we take on in leadership is not always our own. It is more likely to be the sharing of someone else's load, whether of illness, bereavement, or pain resulting from sinful actions. Paul advises, 'Brothers, if someone is caught in a sin, you who are spiritual should restore him gently. But watch yourself, or you also may be tempted. Carry each other's burdens, and in this way you will fulfil the law of Christ' (Galatians 6:1–2). Sometimes it is easy to over-identify with the needy person. I well remember waking up in anguish one night imagining that I was a prisoner in a tiny upstairs room, unable to walk or move one step. In fact, I was only living through the pain and frustration of little Annie Hall, a woman who lived in our parish and belonged to one of our women's groups in the church, who had recently suffered a double amputation in order to save her life. Without legs, she spent many hours alone in her upstairs room, free only to pray and pour out love on all who visited her. By over-identifying I had taken her pain to myself in a way that destroyed my sleep with imagined fears, which only hindered me in bearing her burdens in a positive and creative way. For me that was an early lesson in pastoral care. If it was possible to be drained of energy and disqualified from serving *one* person adequately, through over-much sympathy, the problem could only be magnified as ministry extends to more and more people.

The secret in pastoral care is to remember that 'I' am not the answer to everyone's needs. Although I am being changed from one degree of glory to another, I am still at best a weak person seeking to bring God's strength to others. Paul speaks of those who minister as 'jars of clay' (2 Corinthians 4:7). We have 'this ministry' not because of our ability, but because of 'God's mercy' (2 Corinthians 4:1). We have the treasure of the gospel and the presence of Christ, the light of the world, in the 'earthen vessels' of our frail human lives, 'to show that this all-surpassing power is from God and not from us' (v 7).

It is a power that enables us to bring people out of Satan's darkness into Christ's light (v 4) and it is a ministry that brings us into an experience of suffering that is not explained only in terms of the pain of those to whom we minister. There is the cost of a wider conflict between good and evil that involves pressure, persecution and attack upon our lives. 'We are hard pressed on every side, but not crushed; perplexed, but not in despair; persecuted, but not abandoned; struck down, but not destroyed' (v 9). This is one of several passages describing the extent of Paul's afflictions in the course of his apostolic ministry, and many of us imagine such sufferings to be unique to his pioneering work for Christ. Those who work among Christians imprisoned for their faith in various parts of the world will realise that twentieth century Christians are not exempt from suffering equally severe torments. What many do not realise is that the conflict with the powers of evil is so sharp today that many who are engaged in small group leadership can expect to endure personal hardship, particularly as they seek to help those who have been previously engaged in some form of occult practice.

But none should be deterred from such ministry because it is difficult. Paul, having received 'this ministry', is not surprised that it is costly to follow in the way of Christ: 'We always carry around in our body the death of Jesus' (literally, 'the dying of Jesus'), 'so that the life of Jesus may also be revealed in our body. For we who are alive are always being given over to death for Jesus' sake, so that his life may be revealed in our mortal body' (2 Corinthians 4:10–11).

This is the level at which apostolic ministry operates. We think of small group membership or leadership as a commitment to our diaries, or the filling up of a lot of time. We can be rather proud of being chosen to lead. It gives us a certain kudos and an element of status and acceptability. For us it is about committee meetings, planning sessions, Bible study and prayer times. In God's sight it is about eternity entering time, goodness challenging evil, resurrection defeating death, glory being manifested through suffering. We need the dying to self, 'for we do not preach ourselves, but Jesus Christ as Lord, and ourselves your servants for Jesus' sake' (2 Corinthians 4:5). If we are dedicated to the sort of service expressed by Jesus himself, we shall accept all the cost and all the troubles of ministry gladly. We shall see them in the context of eternity, 'for our light and momentary troubles are achieving for us an eternal glory that far outweighs them all' (2 Corinthians 4:17).

Books for further help

ASHTON Cyril
Serving Spirit, Serving Church. London: Marshall Pickering, 1988.

COTTERELL Peter
All About House Groups. Eastbourne: Kingsway, 1985.

GRIGOR Jean
Grow to Love. St Andrews: St Andrews Press, 1980.

MALLISON, John
Growing Christians in small Groups. London: Scripture Union, 1989.

ORTIZ Juan Carlos
Disciple. London: Lakeland, 1976.

PATTISON Stephen
A Critique of Pastoral Care. London: SCM Press, 1988.

PEACE, Richard
Small Group Evangelism. London: Scripture Union, 1987.

POINTER, Roy
(foreword)
Good Things Come in Small Groups. London: Scripture Union, 1987.

SUMMERTON, Neil
A Noble Task – Eldership and Ministry in the Local Church. Exeter: Paternoster Press, 1987.